I0233702

SPIRITUAL WARFARE

The Fight, The Freedom, The Fire

Sandra Cerda

Spiritual Warfare: *The Fight the Freedom the Fire* © 2015, 2018, 2021 by Sandra Cerda, All Rights Reserved.

ISBN-10: 0692364560

ISBN-13: 978-0692364567

COVER DESIGN: Sandra Cerda and Kevron2001

BOOK INTERIOR DESIGN: Sandra Cerda for New Life Publishing

©2015, 2018, 2021 All Rights Reserved.

No portion of this literature may be reproduced either written or implied without the expressed written permission of the copyright owner. Use of this literature may be referred to in writing for brief quotations so long as notice of the copyright owner appears on the title or copyright page of the work as follows:

Taken from the book: Spiritual Warfare: *The Fight the Freedom the Fire* © 2015 by Sandra Cerda, All Rights Reserved. Used by permission.

Scripture taken from THE AMPLIFIED BIBLE/Old Testament Copyright © 1965, 1987 by the Zondervan Corporation. The Amplified New Testament Copyright © 1958, 1987 by the Lockman Foundation. Used by Permission.

References made from the Webster's New World College Dictionary, Fourth Edition © 1999 by Macmillan USA All Rights Reserved. Printed in the United States of America.

New Life Publishing

Bringing 1st Time Authors to Print!

On Facebook @1st Time Authors

For the men and women of God
who are *quickly* learning what it means
to *hold the line.*

CONTENTS

SECTION THREE
The Fire: *Holiness*   87

For years,
I failed to know who the real enemy was.
I am forever grateful to the men and women of God
who continue to preach *the demonstrated*
word of God with a fierce heart,
for **His Truth.**

My eyes are <u>forever</u> opened.

FROM THE AUTHOR

I was lured into the world of witchcraft and sorcery, through the lie that there is a difference between white and black magic. There is no difference.

Witchcraft is witchcraft and separates you from God.

My husband was raised in the occult. Grandparents on both sides of his family were drenched in it and like how we dedicate our children to the Lord, his grandfather dedicated him as a child, to *Satan.*

But God had another plan.

Sickness had consumed the entirety of my body; all my skin was infected from head to toe, and my hair was falling out. I was desperate. With over ten doctors, and multiple tests, after 30 months I was referred to the University of Texas Health Science Center for further *testing and diagnosis.* I was to be a guinea pig. I was pregnant with my youngest son.

Infection had worsened, and before my son turned six months old, all hope was gone. I found myself walking toward the altar of a very large church, one early Sunday morning; I needed a miracle. I had been so lost for so long. There were no more doctors I could turn to; the diagnosis was the same.

But God had another plan.

I was about to be set free. I did not know I was full of devils. I did not know anything about the reality of that world, only that I had played in it for a pretty good while. Ignorance will take you **through hell, and *to hell*,** if you let it.

Spiritual Warfare is real. The world of spirits is a very real world, *even tangible, and audible.* We live in a world of worlds with the rise of evil increasing mightily, and with great horror and brutality. There is no end in sight, yet our hope and strength are from the Lord, and so we endure.

"Not only so, but we also glory in our sufferings, because we know that suffering produces perseverance, perseverance produces character, and character produces hope. And hope does not put us to shame, because God's love has been poured out into our hearts through the Holy Spirit, who has been given to us." Romans 5:3-5

The Lord has revealed truths to me, which I had on some occasions heard from the mouths of His anointed but had never really taken to heart. In other words, the **reality** of these great truths remained hidden from me by my fear of walking in the *Light* of them **by faith in God.**

The time had now come though, when the Lord began to impress me that, *"due season is due, and the time is **now** where seeds that have been planted in your heart and life must bear fruit; they must yield increase."*

It is a matter of walking through *impossible* circumstances and situations, with only your trust in the Lord. That is what a hint of spiritual warfare is, because you must agree with the Spirit of God, that the spirit of fear has no place in you and the spirit of faith prevails in your life.

To obtain this level of increase and growth in maturity, *hunger, and thirst for more of God, such as you have never known before in your life,* **will alone** get you there. It comes through great trials and testing, challenges in life and even the threat of attack through its many forms.

A hunger and thirst; a desperation that reaches their parched peak, as the Psalmist wrote, *"in a dry and weary land where no water is" (Psalm 63:1),* knowing that God alone can meet your need, and will.

Learning and accepting I was no longer as a child *needing milk, (Hebrews 5:12- 14),* continuing out of necessity in the basics of His Word, His will and His way led to a great enabling. Too much milky stuff runs right through you; makes a person weak. God wants to bulk us up with the meat of His Word, revealing itself through us! I am all for God bulking me up! That is where the strength, *enabling strength*, is found!

We are **enabled by the Spirit of God** to *proceed in advanced teachings (Hebrews 6:3), which in turn causes an increase to our faith.* Enabled to *experience the demonstration*, the result, of great spiritual breakthroughs in life. The Spirit of God will teach you what *NO MAN* can teach you.

My prayer is that you are <u>informed and challenged</u> by the teaching of this material, to do all and then some, of what God has anointed you to do, but to do so by a faith that is informed, seasoned and skilled in handling His Word. For we are in a day where the Lord is **growing us up** fast!

Many are called **but not fulfilling their call,** for fear they will make a mistake. You will! You will make many, many mistakes. That is where the perfection of Jesus Christ is applied to your life, and experience is forged in the realm of the spirit. It is part of the process; the proceeding through and toward what only the Holy Spirit can teach.

His calling on your life is irrevocable (Romans 11:29). His purpose prevails. His anointing goes forth; whether you answer the call to be a bearer and imparter of His anointing is determined by your releasing and activating your faith in Him; it is not you are doing anything but believing in Him and living as though you do. Continuing to increase in this area empowers you to walk in a level of God's anointed presence that shatters the hold of the enemy, cancels and thwarts evil assignments **designed and sent** by the devil, himself.

Yes, there is a devil. There is also One Who has total and complete power over his works when we live our lives in accordance with God's will. God has a mission to accomplish, and you can live your life worthy of the assignment you have been destined to walk, in helping to fulfill this mission.

It is a mission of the demonstration of His power in your life, in defeating the works of darkness. We are numbered among those who are not only called, but chosen, to do exactly that. We are anointed, appointed, and approved by the Lord to accomplish our mission, throughout our journey in this life. His hand is on our lives to do it!

We will learn and discover many things on this journey; one very main discovery is in your relationship to the Lord, and its effect. You will be effected by Him. That effect will set men free.

Answer the call today, to learn all you can in this life about how God desires to work through you in this *war of the spirits.*

How to recognize destructive patterns, and their root origins. How and when to engage in spiritual warfare, and the effective forms of engagement. How to teach our children, and why these things occur through the generations. These topics and much more are shared in the pages of this manual.

We need to learn the dangers of ungodly soul ties, how they are formed, how to undo them and live free from their return.

There is a whole world, a kingdom of darkness, ruled by a defeated enemy who keeps our loved ones bound through ignorance and deception. That kingdom is waiting to be overthrown in the *war of the spirits.*

The *hold of the devil* will break as you increase in the knowledge of God and of all that is supplied for us through His word in utilizing it to free our families.

I stood at the gate of death over 30 years ago and all I had were these keys; these truths about God's provision. I am healed and delivered today because I used the keys.

The information in this book will serve as keys in unlocking the door to great victories in liberating our loved ones.

It is time for breakthrough!

SPIRITUAL WARFARE

SECTION ONE

The Fight: *Spiritual Warfare*

I found myself facing the literal fight for my life.

In the mid to late eighty's, I quickly began to experience a rapid, downward spiral of great acceleration, upon implementing a few simple changes in my life.

With as little as three things I began to do differently, I realized I was suddenly out of control in every area of my life, but not until it was too late, *and I was nearly dead.*

Those three things were (1) sexual sin, (2) use of drugs, and (3) practice of witchcraft and sorcery. A triple cord not quickly recognized; *not quickly broken.*

It is no secret that God does not wink at sexual sin; I had heard about adultery all my life. Living with someone you are not married to opens doors to all sorts of chaos and disorder. The blessing of God is far from your relationship until you make it right. With God, you either get right or you get left, as in *behind.*

Going from casual marijuana use, to using over $500 a day of cocaine, was a bondage all its' own and was also *only part of what made my other issues worse*, increasing the bondage on my life a thousand-fold. Then there was the alcohol. Gallons and gallons of it. It was still, only part of my fall.

It was when I opened the door to witchcraft, that sealed my fate and unleashed an assault of evil against me, and those I loved. I was not only hurting myself, but now I was causing great harm to others. It is the sin of rebellion toward God, directly.

The practice of witchcraft will take you through **hell and to hell.** So will rebellion.

First Samuel 15:23 states, *"For rebellion is as the sin of witchcraft, and stubbornness is iniquity and idolatry. Because thou hast rejected the word of the LORD, he hath also rejected thee from being king."*

The word iniquity means *"guilt worthy of punishment."* Iniquity is **the fullness of sin**, *expressed.* Iniquity is birthed through continual meditation and focus of the object of sin. Ability or desire to resist gradually become completely non- existent.

Before long, it is not only a sin that lives in your thoughts, because of your constant focus of it, but soon enough you find yourself DOING IT. You have given *life* to the sins of your *thoughts.* When we flirt with sin, we flirt with lies. Lies that assure us of our ability to control ourselves and the sin.

When we deliberately push away from **inner warnings to cease from sinning** and make things right, we are choosing to give ourselves over to a sinful lifestyle; ***we are committing iniquity.*** Submitting to what we know to be sin, and the sin itself has become our god rather than the Lord.

It was those years during this time, **before I met the Lord and renounced all those sins**, and years following that prompts me to write what the Lord has taught me, concerning the subject of *Spiritual Warfare.*

Had I not passed through those years, I would not have gained the personal insight and firsthand experience that I have gained; had my husband not been exposed to such a painful childhood, surrounded by both white and black magic, he could not have gained the insight and experience that he uses now, in exposing the enemy through *Spiritual Warfare.*

We would not be able to see how craftily, and how subtle it has gained access into the church, behind the pulpit and over the people of God, ultimately into our Christian homes.

It was for the glory of God, that we passed through; endured, although not knowing, it was all part of God's plan.

Over the years, I have ministered about my personal testimony and the restoration of my soul, fiercely and **unashamed**. This freedom from shame has served to usher in great moves of the Holy Spirit leading to physical, spiritual, inner, and emotional healing as well as the healing of the soul, in the lives of others. Transparency. The fight to be transparent before God and man, wars within; we all cover up something. But the Lord should hold that place as *covering*. We say He does; *but does He really?*

As my *covering*, God would have rule over *uncovering* as well; power to reveal; battle scars, healed wounds… He showed His own, and even allowed a doubter named Thomas to **touch the place of the wound**. Healing from doubt followed.

Experiencing divine healing from a painful, most agony filled illness of long duration, and deliverance from bondages well rooted in my soul, offered up lifelong gratitude to my Healer, but not without adversity.

There will always be adversity. The Word of God reveals the Adversary, the devil, assuring us of that adversity and yet we slack up. We stop testifying. The devil wants to stop you from testifying. When we are fervent in God, we testify of His goodness and allow others to see and feel what God has done for us. When God can use you to allow others to touch the place of your wounds, many will be healed from doubt and unbelief.

When doubt and unbelief are around,

miracles are not!

Be fervent to testify ALL that God has done for you, and people will be healed. It was because of unbelief that Jesus could do no miracles, in a certain place (Mark 6:5, Matt. 13:58). *I do not want to live in a place where doubt lives.*

How easy it is to "slack up", and how long it takes to recover from those lapses of fervency toward God. The devil of your soul looks for those gaps; those times when we are too passive or settled in our ways.

I do not know about others, but I simply cannot go a day without spending time in the presence of the Lord. In growing and increasing in the knowledge of God, and learning through trial and error, I and my family have overcome evil attacks made against our lives, family, health, finances, marriage, relationships, church, and ministry. Increasing in the knowledge of God and practicing His presence, affects literally every area of a person's life. His presence is His power, *which creates.*

The Fight ~ The Freedom ~ The Fire

The *fight* of spiritual warfare, the *freedom* and deliverance that comes from spiritual warfare, and the *fire* of the Holy Spirit that results from spiritual warfare, are all included in this warfare manual.

A life of holiness results from living with the knowledge of your God and His love, and the knowledge of your enemy and his defeat. A knowledge that comes from experiencing God in all His glory as his enemies are defeated, by warfare prayer, right before your eyes.

When I turned my back on the way I had been living, and turned to follow the Word, Will and Way of God little did I know that the battle lines were drawn, and the real fight was on.

> *A fight worth having. A freedom worth living.*
> *A fire worth knowing.*

For every believer, **whether you believe it or not,** our life as a Christian on the face of the earth, <u>is a spiritual battle.</u> We are not out of it yet, and preachers who preach a relaxed position against the reality of the devil in our world, are spineless ***delusionist's,*** breeding a watered down, ineffective gospel that leaves people bound, confused, disillusioned, misinformed and therefore ineffective themselves.

They are puppets in the hands of a compromised, half-in, half-out walk with God, that keeps God's people walking with a limp.

Preachers who have become confident in the god of self and fatted by the offerings from God's people? I have seen it with my own eyes.

We are in a war of *spirits*.

1

DISCIPLINED, ORGANIZED & COMMITTED: *THE FORCES OF HELL*

The enemy of God's people takes his position against us, very seriously. So seriously that he has cunningly formed his forces like the ranking of troops in a battalion. He is disciplined. He is organized. He is committed.

Perhaps after serious consideration, you will realize too, that much if not all the Scriptures are written from the viewpoint of a battle: a war in which good battles evil, confrontation is steady, and evil is prevalent in the minds and hearts of people who have no reverence or holy fear of God. It is the tug of war between flesh and spirit, with the soul of man in the balance.

Ultimately though, true holiness overcomes ungodliness through the power of unity between man and the Spirit of God.

In this issue of unity, again we see that this is where the power lies, **and the enemy knows it.**

The enemy of your soul believes in the power of unity and knows all too well that *through this force* oppositions cannot prevail against the other. Only through either fear, exhaustion, fatigue, or works of the flesh such as sin and compromise, can the adversary of your soul find a foothold. The weakness of our flesh is evident in our daily lives, such as outbursts of emotions like rage, or the constant *giving in* to people, or behavior that *YOU KNOW* is contrary to your own standards, and the Lord's.

The overwhelming force of the Holy Spirit, the shed Blood of Christ's body, and the penetrating, infallible Word of God working in the life of the Spirit filled believer, are all powerful; *powerful enough to change everything.*

The *key* though, is unwavering belief and unswerving unity with God.

The Spirit of Unity spoken of in the book of Ephesians is brought about by the binding force of peace.

"Be eager and strive earnestly to guard and keep the harmony and oneness of, and produced by, the Spirit in the binding power of peace"
Ephesians 4:3

In another translation,

"...endeavoring to keep the unity of the Sprit in the bond of peace"

It is the *absence of being unified* with God's **plan and purpose** for our lives, that hinders the flow, and steady progress of the Holy Spirit *(in our lives and in the lives of others)*. It is the one thing that keeps churches from growing.

Lack of unity keeps disorder, and confusion very busy. Lack of unity is the gut of discord and division, and is kept strong through murmuring, backbiting and discontent.

An individual, who is not walking in unity with the Spirit of God in their lives is either fighting

God, themselves, or something *[some force].* The same holds true for every church.

God works through many means to get through to us, for the ultimate purpose of our healing and our wholeness, spirit, soul, and body, and in unifying us for His purpose. One of the things, or issues He works toward is our freedom from anger, with roots in unforgiveness, *stemming from betrayal.*

Allowing forgiveness to take place in life, makes room for *God's perfect peace* to carve a path toward one's healing. Whether it is that a person is fighting God *[at war with God in their spirit]*, or something else, the only way to overcome the devil is to position ourselves, align our lives, in order with God's word. Submit, yield, and surrender to **God's word, God's Will, and God's Way,** and be made whole.

I have known of people leaving their church because the congregation spent too much time in worship or in prayer; *"too needy"*, they said.

I had a couple tell me over fifteen years ago, that members of our congregation would cry during the worship portion of the church service because they were "too messed up and didn't want to get better."

This same couple left our church, took those same weeping, *"messed up"* members and started their own church, in a laughter movement they called *"the river of joy"*. In an email to me later, the husband of the two wrote referring to these believers in the Lord Jesus Christ, as *"misfits"*. In less than five years they quit the church, and left the people with no pastor or covering, so their daughters could pursue a singing and dancing career in the world of Country & Western style, *Christian music*. Apparently, God had changed His mind about them pastoring a church.

Divisive. Judgmental. Prideful. Trickster. Haughty. Vain. Deceiving, Church Splitting, shameless Proselyting Preachers... and more; all in one couple who sat in our congregation strategizing how to pick our church apart.

We were about to learn spiritual warfare on a whole new level. The devil on this level was IN the church, literally. Involved **in and with** the unsuspecting members of the church. Involved **in and with** the financial details of the church, and one of the largest givers of financial support to the church. So confident in his money that he attempted bribes in the multiple tens of thousands of dollars, for a leadership position that would allow him pulpit access. The only problem is that he had questionable habits, for the sake of *"closing business deals" in public relations for his day trading job.; he entertained in sexually oriented businesses, daily.*

When he quickly discovered we, as pastors were not for sale, and our pulpit could not be *"bought"*, he led many families out, and against us. It was one of the first major blows to our ministry, and lives. There were multiple others.

Those who *sabotage;* planting themselves right smack in the middle of church life with church members, and almost immediately begin to diagnose the church, the pastors, leaders, and members, attempting to filter in their personal remedies. We had only been pastoring for a few months and had never experienced people who call themselves *Christ- like* to do these things and do it in the Name of Jesus. God does not break down one church, to build up another.

God's nature is to gather, not scatter. There are people who come in and out of my church **right now**, *inviting* people *to go visit* their church. People whose lives have been tremendously affected by our ministry, faithful to this church, and completely unaware of the deception and division behind the invitation.

I am aware of pastors who have built their congregations by thinning out other churches, deliberately going out of their way to do so. These churches fail every time. These pastors are in error, and the fruit of it comes forth without fail.

That is divisive all by itself. If you are guilty of doing it, STOP in the Name of Jesus. If you know someone who is used of the devil to lure people out of their church, STOP THEM, in love but in firmness according to God's word.

The people of God should work **deliberately on the _degrees_** of **Discipline, Organization and Commitment** that they hold toward the church and pastors where God is working to *cover them, speak into their lives, and teach them* God's truths. Pastors are falling prey to exhaustion, because of the outrageous demands and overbearing expectations placed on them; and the constant watching for *wolf-ish*, sinister ministers clothed as sheep, **worming** their way into the church. Cover your pastors!

We ought to pray for our churches, as much as we proclaim to pray, but not as a casual, passive Christian; pray as one who is taught.

Pray for them and demonstrate God's word through **evidence** of a faith filled life; one who *is not hesitant* to **go the extra mile** for their church, by disciplined faith, organized and committed faith. One who *is not hesitant* to **give the extra gift,** and not count it against a church **that is demonstrating the supernatural gifts of the Holy Spirit.** These are churches where the Holy Spirit is actively involved in our day-to-day lives, challenging us through opportunities to stretch our faith in God; to reach the heavens with our faith in a God Who is well-able.

*Evidence, of not just facing hardships but recovering from them, **by faith in God.***

Instead, God's people have divided interests and diverse loyalties vying for their devotion. We are too easily distracted, and often insensitive to the promptings of the Holy Spirit to *come away and learn from Him.* We miss many, many opportunities to tap into the anointing of God's timing for a fresh Word from heaven; **these are strategic promptings the Lord is executing,** and many Christians are missing them.

We lack discipline and most especially (1) *self-discipline.* This is the open door to (2) a lack of organization in our lives, and finally to (3) little or no commitment.

Disciplined. Organized. Committed

The forces of hell can do it successfully, yet God's people struggle, *not for lack of provision or ability,* but for lack of activation of God's word in their lives. Lack of endurance.

Knowing the Word is not enough;
we are responsible for living out *by example and*
demonstrating our faith in what we know
of our God and of His Word.

God does not

break down

one church, to

build up another.

DECIDE & DECREE:
DECLARING SPIRITUAL WARFARE

W hen you decide to walk by faith, when you decide to rest in the Lord, when you decide to stand after you have done all to stand, **you have declared war, in the spirit.**

When you make up your mind that God's word for your life, family and future is the Standard you are going to live by, **you have declared war, in the spirit.**

Everything changes when war has been declared both in this world *and in the unseen world.*

There is no changing your mind halfway through, there is no switching sides or letting up in your declaration once your decision has been made.

An official order given by a person of power or authority, is a decree. When we, as God's people in faith decide and decree, we are declaring **by order of our authority in Christ,** that all evil activity, assignments, workings, and the like, are to cease and desist *immediately*, in the Name of Jesus Christ, by the Power of the Blood of Jesus. Our authority comes from the Lord.

By enforcement of God's word and our authority to operate in it, we do not deter from this decision, decree, or declaration *until we see the evidence of prayer being answered*, and that

God's order has been implemented.

Where we find disorder, *we implement through spiritual warfare,* God's Divine Order, and we do our part as God's people to maintain that Order.

Where we find illness, *we implement through spiritual warfare,* God's goodness, and healing. Where there is chaos, *by prayer, not passive prayer either but prayer with authority given by God,* we implement God's Peace.

Recently, I was part of a powerfully charged, fully yielded to the Lord, group of women ministering at a Women's Conference, in Houston, Texas. Every aspect of this gathering was about deciding, decreeing, and declaring over our lives, and the lives of those we love dearly. Some decisions were the first steps toward newness of life, as women gave their hearts to Jesus for the very first time. Others, who love the Lord gathered to help women make the decisions that day; decisions that brought life altering change to us, as women.

Declarations made over specific illnesses, diseases, and sicknesses, *powerfully brought those things to nothing* that day, as women gathered in a united faith. Recognizing and removing *by the power of God,* those things that have kept them, their children and loved ones bound, women rose with one heart, mind, voice, spirit, soul, and body, **and prospered.**

We declared spiritual warfare over our sons and daughters, *and theirs* to a thousand generations, *(Exodus 20:6, Deut. 7:9, Psalm 105:8), reminding God of His promise to us, concerning them.* A power greater than ourselves surged through us reaching the very throne room of God, WHILE OUR LOVED ONES WERE STRUGGLING IN SIN.

We forgot to mope about it. We forgot to whine and fret to our "prayer-partner" about it, repetitiously and in vain. We forgot, long enough to act on our faith in God...suddenly, we, as **one body**, agreed *and in one accord* with the will of heaven for our lives.

For some, many, and probably ALL of us, there was turmoil happening somewhere in the life of a loved one; *of someone who was far from God and getting farther fast.* Perhaps the turmoil of a horrible medical report, or the fear of a looming divorce. Turmoil comes in many shapes, sizes, and forms.

Turmoil is a weapon that forms against us; against our lives and the lives of the people we love the most.

When a daughter does not come home, the turmoil starts through your concerns and fears. When a son revolts against his father, you know there is about to be GREAT turmoil. When those things the Lord has shown you of your children are the farthest thing, you are able to see them doing, living and being... you are in turmoil about it.

If you are not careful, you will entangle yourself in the *emotional part* of your battle and become completely ineffective in the **spiritual part** of it. That is how you know you are losing the battle; you are too emotionally involved and therefore, are not achieving the successful results that come from <u>Effective Spiritual Warfare.</u>

Effective Spiritual Warfare **creates** a shift. *Effective Spiritual Warfare* **causes** an acceleration. For some the acceleration is good, and for others *it is bad.*

For those who are living in the fullness of God for their lives, the acceleration is good, with healthy challenges and outcomes. Good things begin to happen, with great acceleration. As if the Lord is bringing us up to speed, and we find ourselves **in step with God** and His blessings, such as answered prayers.

For those who are living **outside of God's fullness** for their lives, the acceleration is not so good. It is as if they are stuck, and nothing good is happening. They have no joy. They have no inward peace. They experience a continual dissatisfaction with life, with family, with anything to do with commitment. It is as if one bad thing after another, with no end in sight continually bombards those who are outside of God's blessing.

God knows how to get our attention, by working through the bad choices we make, and gives us extended opportunity to make things right. When we notice our loved ones, who do not have God in their lives *at all or completely,* begin to suffer these hard accelerations, KEEP PRAYING! God will bring them through, and ALL THE WAY.

Expect your prayers for your loved ones, to be challenged. Expect the Adversary to work adverse situations, and adversity in every form through people you love, to STOP you from praying *effectively.*

Spiritual warfare is a <u>fight.</u>

It is a fight, **not against people** but against devils who keep them *enslaved* to a life of evil, suffering, lack and confusion. **It is a fight FOR people,** and not *against them.* When you know who your enemy is, the fight **with** people *stops*.

Too often God's people imagine that they can engage effectively, but they fail in the very middle of the fight for lack of preparation.

Preparation **ONLY** comes through spending time alone, with God; *and the devil knows it. Preparation includes being an **active, servant of the Lord** in your local church, and to the pastor God has **given you**.* God **gives** you a pastor. You do not get to pick your own. You will pick a Saul when God is giving you a David. One after **His own** heart!

*Preparation comes from continual sacrificing of the needs and the wants of your**self**, because your**self** and the self-ish, self -centered issues of life will always want to be the priority. Only God can remain the Priority. The things of God, which include the local church He has planted you in, should be at the center of your heart, along with all other important things to you. A thought life filled with hopes, prayers and concerns for the same things God cares for is a sign of a Godly, God-Centered life.* The call of a pastor is a spiritual one, not requiring gender or certification by man. Those, and other non-biblical restrictions imposed by some religious mindset leaves out the Holy Spirit. The anointing of God determines the functionality and confirms the office of the man or woman of God **He** has chosen. God sees the heart, not their gender. God qualifies you, not man. Man can confirm the calling of God on your life, but man is not your filter and should not be given power over your calling. This is a spiritual weight and battle unnecessarily imposed over God's people. Shame.

We need all **hands-on-deck!** Check your heart and get busy about your father's business! We should be stepping-stones not stumbling blocks.

Why do I state that the center of our heart and thought life should include the church and pastors God has for your life? For one reason, it is, where the lost can be brought to hear God's word and be freed; be saved. The heart of God is for the salvation of the lost that comes by and through the preaching of His Word and the Presence of His Holy Spirit. Being mindful, considerate and a caring servant of God toward the church and pastors, protects the anointing that results in won souls.

Another reason is because it is where the Altar of the Lord is, our place of intimate worship. Worship that ushers in our healing and wholeness. Those things of God, that our families need so desperately.

When you learn *to protect* the anointing of God,

God will bless you for it. When you learn to *recognize why* the devil keeps trying to get you out of your church, you will stop listening and entertaining the idea of another pasture. God gives us wisdom in spiritual insight, as we mature toward the things of God.

My version or understanding of Matthew 6:33 is this: *Seek first the Kingdom of God (the things of God), and all its righteousness (and all the things that are right and good in relation to the Kingdom of God) … and all these things (our personal needs and that of our loved ones), will be added to us (will be given to us as a blessing to our faith in this).* In other words, God will take care of those personal issues, when we have put His issues, first.

People are added to the church and multiplied to the church, according to the pattern of the Holy Spirit in the book of Acts, when priority remains priority.

It is the first step to our being adequately prepared for the spiritual warfare we must be actively aware of. It is first base.

You shall also decide and decree a thing, and it shall be established for you; and the light of God's favor shall shine on your ways. Job 22:27,28

Effective Spiritual Warfare **creates** *a shift.*

3
THE POWER OF SIMPLE
OBEDIENCE

Your simple obedience to God, in your life as shown by your *Example-Christianity*, is a declaration of war, in the realm *or world* of the spirit.

Early in my Christian life I quickly learned that every form of obedience to God's word produced a *"stirring"* in the spirit world or an *"upset"* to those things or people around me who were antagonistic toward the things of God, or the true and accurate direction of God for specific situations.

Often, when it came to people, it was not the person but an *"underlying overtone, or mood"* that would change. The atmosphere would change.

One example has to do with obedience while in great transition, when no sign of an end is in sight.

God's word teaches that we are to **hold our ground** when there is nothing else to do, or any other **God given direction**. There is always something you can do, *but it may not necessarily be at the direction of the Lord*, or in the direction of His leading.

You make a lot of people angry, and even frustrated at you, when you fail to take their advice, heed their warnings, or follow their direction... many who have imagined themselves to be spiritually mature, have no clue that they are not. Others who imagine that age is a factor that equals seniority, are ruffled to learn they are wrong when it comes to the things of God, and of spiritual leadership and ability.

They lack the experience to pastor people, and often attempt to *pastor the pastor.* Get those people out of your church, in the Name of Jesus! *and quick!*

Hold the position of faith before God and man. When you have heard from the Lord on a particular subject or situation, and everything and everyone around you is falling short, giving up, exhausted, cannot see clearly, cannot handle it anymore, disagrees with you, turns on you, takes people out of your church to "protect" them from you, whispers against you... *BUT YOU KNOW YOU HEARD FROM THE LORD,* **stand.**

Hold the line.

Do not make a move, if God is not the one moving you. Simple obedience to the simple things the Lord directs us to do, **is warfare.** All hell will come against you to get you to make just ONE MOVE outside of God's directive.

Do not do it.

Do not give in to the counsel of man, to the desperation of your own thoughts or *"ways" that* might help things happen faster...

Do not give in to the frustrations and impatience of others who love the Lord, or to their selfish pressuring of you to DO SOMETHING.

Hold the line. Stand your ground.

Keep your position.

God's word teaches us how we are to avoid beginning in the Spirit and ending in the flesh (Galatians 3:3).

People who have claimed they will be with you through thick and thin, because GOD sent them to you... will be defined by simple acts of obedience or their lack of them.

Settle your faith to believe God for the impossible. He is waiting on you to believe that He can do that which is currently, *impossible to you.*

God is waiting on you to believe that He can do superabundantly, *far over and above all* you could *ever hope for, think of, dream of, or imagine.* He is the God of the *impossible,* and He is *able and willing* to bring you through every trouble that you face. **He is God!**

We have had our hearts broken over the most immature doings of seemingly mature Christians, who demand a respect that has not been earned. People *who stoop so low* as to *pull out* innocent family members from what the Lord is doing in their lives at our church. When these same people cannot get their way, which is a way that leads to error, they go the extra mile to justify themselves in some warped way and split the church. The only result is hurt people, confused, and displaced.

It is the fruit of disobedience; a disobedience to sound instruction, and to being still and trusting the Lord. The Lord is in the simple things, like *"stand when you've done all to stand."*

I believe the Lord seeks out those who will be so bold as to trust the still small voice of the Lord, in the heat of the battle. There is a powerful force from heaven to be experienced when the storm is in full force, and the voices of many are loud and lifted and **suddenly,** because of your <u>developed relationship with God</u>, you hear His voice.

You obtain from the Lord, strategy, through simple obedience to God. Strategy is defined as *the art of planning and directing overall military operations and movements in a war or battle.*

You obtain tactic from the Lord as well, through *simple obedience* to God, to His Word, His Will, and His Way. Tactic is defined as *the art of disposing armed forces in order of battle and of organizing operations, especially during contact with an enemy.*

Throne room intervention comes from simple obedience to God, and the results are throne room blessings; *breakthroughs in prayer for our lives and those we love.*

Do not let **well-meaning** people get you off track, and out of step with the direction God is leading you. You, yourself, *are **well able*** to hear from the Lord when you are **active in relationship with Him**. Most especially as a pastor in oversight of God's people, you are the one the Lord speaks to regarding them. He can and will and *has* spoken through others but to confirm what the Lord has spoken or shown **you,** as His shepherd.

Do not let **ill-meaning** people get you off track, either. Wolves in sheep clothing, is a term referenced in the Scriptures to describe hidden, evil motives that work through people who come in and out of our churches, with agendas that are self-serving and divisive.

We have had pastors turn on us because we would not come up *"under"* them and allow them to be our *"covering"*, our *"pastor"* and our *"apostle"*. I had one pastor angry because I did not let him *empty a bottle of oil* on my head. Another woman pastor turned on me when I questioned why younger adult men, who wanted to be *"covered" by her apostolic self,* had to kneel, and kiss her feet in homage. **We saw it with our own eyes.**

Pastors have told us to our face that blessings the Lord had granted us, were intended for them. One self-proclaimed prophet told us the Lord was moving us into a more Evangelical ministry that would require us to travel, and we were *to leave the church to him, to pastor while we were away.* He said all that in the Name of Jesus, too!

Another pastor *slandered us* when we did not join his *Mini-Mega Ministry,* whatever that was! Still another pastor, *turned on me* when my husband would not travel to another country with him in his Jonathon Ministry; he ultimately sold his church, and retired in luxury.

When you know God, *you know His ways.* You know the quickening of the Holy Ghost and the warnings that come from the Lord. Heed the warnings of the Lord, in simple obedience.

God has a peculiar way of deliberately blessing those who stay true to His directives, and He does it openly. As if to show doubters and troublers, that He is **very well able** to speak to His pastors directly, and to reward them for their stand.

Settle your **faith** to *believe God* for the impossible.

4

UNFORGIVENESS:

SATAN'S STRONGEST WEAPON

For many people, this is where everything stops. The subject of forgiveness is an extremely sensitive subject, and one that should be handled with great respect to everyone's specific situation, but the *inability* to forgive the trespassing, unjust pain and unfairness inflicted by others, remains Satan's strongest means of power against us.

About forgiveness **of self**, there is a major warring going on, within the very fiber, very soul of a person. This is a tearing of the soul, and a depth only the Lord can reach, touch, and heal. *It takes many seasons of time, and much patience, but wholeness and healing do come.*

So many people are at war with God, in their spirit, about forgiveness. Whether it is the forgiving of another person, or of self, the pain is deeply real. What you hold in the soul, you feel in the body.

To forgive is to open the way for wholeness to make its way through, to the life of the person who is doing the *forgiving.*

For me it was like having a boulder right smack in the middle of the road I was traveling on. The road was my life; the boulder was called Unforgiveness. It was the only thing blocking me from receiving the healing promises of God, for my body. I spoke of this in my book, "Incest: The Curse of Destruction...Reversed". Once that boulder was removed, my healing sprang forth! I had suffered for 30 months of sickness that left nearly 100% of my skin raw, bleeding, infected and foul.

Forgiveness was **my key** *to* **my miracle**!

I was a bitter, angry young woman. For many *good reasons*, I was bitter. For many good *reasons*, I had become angry and defensive. The sin of betrayal made against me as a child, had grown a wiry root of destructive behavior, destructive mindset, and a self-destructive life.

Forgiving the <u>source</u> of my pain, set me free.

Forgiving the man who had raped me as a child, who had sexually assaulted me several times, as a child, was an issue I could no longer ignore.

Not forgiving him had made my life *sick.*

There is so much sickness in the lives of the people of God, as well as those who have chosen not to live for God. Sickness that is often the result of an angry mind, and hardened heart; anger and hardness that result from betrayal. Betrayal that found its way through sin. There is no end *until the moment you release it all* takes place.

That first step <u>is a life-changer.</u>

Often, we nurse grudges, we nurse wounds, we nurse our hurts and they are nursed in the cesspool of a wounded spirit, who refuses to draw near to God, *on His terms*. A wounded spirit working in a person will keep that person *seeing the good as evil, and the evil as good.*

I know about the sickness of un-forgiveness, and the infection of a warring spirit before God.

I also know about the healing power of God that springs forth with strength and hope, life, and real joy when the war against God in your spirit, ceases; when you ask Him to **help you want to** forgive... when you ask Him to take away the very real feelings, and very **just and righteous reasons** for your anger, for your un-forgiveness...

I have wrestled with the Lord over some very real, very deeply painful issues and circumstances. Situations that have unfairly taken over areas of my life, through the actions and ugliness of others. Situations completely un-called for, unfair, and wrong, where there was nothing, I could do to change it; *except to forgive.*

As recently as one month ago, I stood at the casket of the man who had inflicted the most horrible pain and betrayal of trust any man could inflict against a child. Far worse when the child *is family*. Forty-seven years had passed.

Surrounded by people who blamed me for exposing what he had done; *for crying out as a victim.* His family: people who loved him. People who had never been hurt by him, who had never known him to be aggressive or at all capable of sexually assaulting a four-year-old child. But he did.

Although there was a great mix of emotion, and

tensions at the funeral brought on by other unexpected circumstances, *I had peace.* I had already buried this pain years before when I embraced God's definition of forgiveness.

God's definition of forgiveness is so completely opposite of what I ever believed it was. Upon accepting Jesus Christ as Savior and Lord, in a way and in a manner outlined in His Word, I learned that forgiveness was a major issue to God. *I quickly learned that it was a major issue to me as well.*

The weapon the enemy was successfully using against me was an unforgiving mind and heart. I thought <u>avoiding the subject</u> was a sign of my forgiveness, but in truth when the subject was brought forward from time to time my initial response was inner sadness; *<u>then rage.</u>*

Inwardly I held and covered the truth of my wounds and how deeply they ran, from the people I loved most and interacted with in my daily life; making me nothing more than a wounded, angry person who did not like herself very much...

Part of God's equipping me, was through my initial life cleansing experience called True Forgiveness: the kind that drops you to your knees.

The kind that *issues out* and *pours out* the innermost truths of our grief, anger, resentment, unwillingness, and rigidity, as only one who is being dealt with by God, can experience.

Only God's definition of forgiveness results in the springing forth of healing, and His anointing to heal others, *through you.*

Satan's strongest weapon against you, is suddenly destroyed; useless, and brought to nothing. It is brought to *NO EFFECT*.

You are suddenly equipped with a *super,* supernatural ability to experience healing in multiple dimensions: inwardly, outwardly and extending to others. You are now effective in the ability to connect people to the same Healer you have connected with, through simple, life-transforming forgiveness.

Had I not yielded to the Lord, **His right-of-way** in bringing me through an unforgiving life, I would not have been able to demonstrate victory at the foot of my attacker's coffin.

Victory over hate. Victory over anger. Victory over vengeance. Victory over resentment.

I leaned into his coffin, the first time, and kissed his cheek. I cried like a little girl who did not know what she had done wrong, to have had this happen to her. **Why me?** It nearly destroyed my life, what he had done to me. It literally destroyed any family ties that would have otherwise been forged in great love. He took all of that and so much more, away from me, away from my children and grandchildren as well.

"Why", would *never* be answered.

The next morning, I made sure I was the last one to stand before his casket. I took the opportunity to seal the last words ever to be spoken into his ear. My voice was the last voice to ever speak into his ear.

I leaned in again, kissed his cheek, with only a single tear left running down my face, and whispered my heart to him, before God:

I love you,

and

I forgive you.

Walking away, I turned again to see the casket being closed. That chapter of my life was truly over, now. I knew I had been freed.

Unforgiveness has **_nothing_** in me.

SECTION TWO

The Freedom: Deliverance

Amazing, it is, to think that simple people like you and me can be used for Divine purposes in today's day and age.

Many shun the subject of deliverance; it is after all, the *"messy"* part of Christianity, and not the "glamorous" or "fun" part.

Deliverance, though, when properly administered and functionally operating fully by the Holy Spirit, is swift and not messy. People can be liberated from crippling, demonic oppression, and bondages, from soul ties and familiar spirits, generational and inherited curses.

There is no better school of deliverance, than the schooling taught by the Lord! No classroom hours spent learning stuff that puts YOU in bondage; just walking out your Christian life in the power and authority of God. Daily.

He came to set the captives free. That sounds like deliverance to me, for those who shun this Act of Freedom by Christ. It is the sign of a liberated soul, when one can liberate another. A sign and a wonder we need to see more of.

To bring God honor and glory by undoing the assignments and works of evil, to reverse the effects of sin through forgiveness, is a great reward for those who work deliverance of captives. Let us bring God even more glory! Let us bring great honor to His Name, by setting captives *free*.

Let us be so bold, and so full of compassion that leads to healing, where demonstration after demonstration increases as evidence of a merciful God, wins people over. It happens when you KNOW the God you serve; the God you belong to, and what you have in Him, as inherited.

It is time now to stir up the gift of God that is in you; the gift that *frees men's souls.*

And such as do wickedly against the covenant shall he corrupt by flatteries; but the people that do know their God shall be strong and do mighty exploits. Daniel 11:32

5

BINDING *FAMILIAR* SPIRITS

This is one of the *easiest spirits* to detect and remove, but *only* from a person who does their part. When God shuts the door, we would do good not to go back and open it.

Christians are easier to fall for a familiar spirit, than many would care to know. It is only for a lack of knowledge God's people continue to fall for these subtle trespassers.

Familiar spirits and generational curses work together. Whether it is old habits or old behavior patterns, the root cause is a returning familiar spirit, or a generational curse attempting to find ground to operate in.

This spirit is also found in many churches, you might be surprised to hear; churches where **the old and the former** are kept alive and honored, at the expense of allowing the Holy Spirit to minister freely to God's people. Churches where tradition with the form and the way of things, supersedes anything that promotes any personal growth in the Holy Spirit. The Holy Spirit is quenched in these churches; *grieved*, as God's word describes it.

Behavior in a person can keep the curse alive and going back to former behaviors can resurrect the curse from the dead.

For example, when an addict who is freed from one addiction, substitutes the first addiction for another addiction, there is a *familiar spirit* involved: and a soul tie to the object of addiction.

We give devils ground to work in, place to operate and occupy within us, whether it comes through our eye-gate, hearing or thoughts which all affect our actions. We roll out a *"welcome mat"* to devils when our choices put us in places where they play.

Addiction is the interaction or relationship with a person or substance *that has mood altering qualities* and **life demanding, life changing and life ending effects.** You can have an addiction to the person you love, and keep going back to that person, no matter how beat and defeated that person leaves you. Regardless of how many broken promises the object of your addiction is guilty of, you keep believing the lie that "it will change". Addiction to anything or anyone, will do that.

A wicked soul tie will do that.

A familiar spirit is derived from the Latin word *familiaris*, which means "household servant", expressing the idea that witches and sorcerers had spirits to obey and serve them, in their craft or work. People who attempt to contact the dead, to this day, have spirit guides who they communicate with. These spirit guides are familiar spirits; demonic, as their source.

Some families have a spirit of Infirmity running through generations in their family, such as cancer or blood diseases, mental or any number of other ills and diseases.

Some families have a spirit of Bondage running through generations in their family, such as incarceration, backsliding, or unbelief such as atheism.

Families have suffered generations of an evil curse such as a barren womb, miscarriages in multiples, and other female issues. These are forms of familiar spirits that go in and out of families seasonally, visiting one generation after another, in search of a place or person to express themselves through; someone who has given them a familiar place to stay and operate its evil through. One description of this type of spirit is found in Luke 11:24,

> *When the unclean spirit is gone out of a man, he walks through dry places, seeking rest; and finding none, he says "I will return to my house from where I came out."*

This is what the devil says about you, about your *family!* That devil is familiar with you, familiar with your family, and your church. With your history and with what unsettles you; what causes you fear. What makes you *"snap'" or* triggers you. Familiar spirits are behind that.

One example, very close to my life, is the time I was violated as a child. The curse of premature sexual activity (forming an ungodly soul-tie), through rape and molestation, entered at the age of four, and came back at the age of 5 through another older child, the age of 6 through a teenager, the age of 12 by another adult, and the age of 14 through a more aggressive rape. All by familiar spirits.

At the age of twelve, without warning, I was

awakened to have a man standing over my bed in nothing more than his underwear. He was the owner of the home my half-sister and I, and my brother were sleeping over in, for the weekend. My stepmother's brother.
It was a long night.

Then there were her other two brothers.

Again, at the age of 14. Skipping school was the only thought my half-sister and I had that day; hanging out with friends was the goal of the day. In a short while I would be drugged by a classmate and taken to an overgrown baseball field, during the offseason. Over a bed of fire ants, I was raped. I remember the tiny airplane flying overhead; it was a clear blue sky.

Break the curse of leaving children unattended to; unsupervised. **Break the curse** of leaving your children for others to raise, *for you.*

Make sure when the devil comes back around looking for a familiar place to land, he finds no place in you, no way to your children, your marriage, or your home. Cover your family with the provisions God has supplied. Prayer and intercession, an alert mind, heart and spirit to the strategies of the devil, and **warfare prayer** in Jesus' Name! Fill your life with God and with His Word and Presence and give NO VACANCY, no room for old opportunities, old ways.

Old ways of living equal old ways of dying.

Take God's word in you, and His authority which works through His Word, and bind all familiar spirits from operating in your family. Break the generational curse that continues to find a way in, the curse of sickness, the curse of bondage and destruction. Cover, soak and saturate your loved ones in the precious Blood of Jesus Christ, and speak God's word of Power, without ceasing, when you pray.

Families do not have to suffer, like they do, if they would only take hold of God's truth concerning our victory over evil. **If only one person in every family would choose to live for God** to the fullest, more homes would experience God's delivering power from evil. More children would have safer homes, safer environments to grow up in. Safer.

If more preachers would get back to the basics of teaching what Jesus taught in most of His teachings, *the defeat of the devil and the demonstration of it,* we would have more victories realized. We would see less people in our churches struggle with warring's of the flesh, and tug-of-wars with the devil.

It starts in the pulpit, and spills over into the homes. It starts with the head of the church and leads to the head of the family.

Get Order *In*, and Disorder *Out!*

Stay away from preachers who teach you to avoid the devil. **Jesus did not avoid the devil; Jesus confronted the devil** every single time, with the Word and Authority of God, **and eliminated**

Satan's presence and hold on the people. *Every single time!*

Spiritual warfare is what Jesus walked in. Entry of the authority of God, and removal of demons and devils, ushers in the healing, delivering power of God; and God is ultimately glorified for it all, Hallelujah! Every Single Time!

You do not have to go around looking for evil spirits; just living life, offers enough opportunities to walk in the power and authority believers have in the Lord. Only a life of sanctification to God, drives them out. Only a life of sanctification to God, keeps them away.

Nothing breathes familiar spirit *in a church* more than *backbiting, gossip, envy, cliques, discontent, strife, and split tongue lies* about the people, the preacher, and his wife. It would be a good idea to take hold of the Lord in all His fullness. Some Christians live with the Lord in their lives, as if they were living with a shacked-up boyfriend. Close all doors to the devil of loneliness and *marry the Lord!* Holiness keeps unclean spirits that are familiar with you from your past, **away.**

Familiar spirits of sexual sin always go for the single Christian. Only when the child of God is committed to their relationship with the Lord, is one kept from those evil lures of temporary pleasure. With married Christians, the attack is the same, but our victory comes also from the reinforcement of our commitment to our marriage, **to our vows before God.** We have a double reinforcement that must be maintained always, at all costs. The devil loves it when God's people end marriages in divorce; there are times, though, when it cannot be avoided for the sake of safety, and fidelity. There are times when it is all out of your control, and the Lord Himself will bring you through that. Through every part of it. Break the curse of divorce!

With *all* familiar spirits, you will know them by the people they show themselves through. Christians and *non-Christians* alike, can experience the troubling presence and activity of familiar spirits, and the devastation they cause.

<u>Other mentions in the Bible that are <u>evidence</u> of the working of a familiar spirit:</u>

Divination (Witchcraft) (Acts 16:16)

Fear (2 Timothy 1:7)

Lying Spirit (1 Kings 22:22-23)

Whoredom Spirit/Love of the World
(Worship of other gods, Hosea 4:12)

Spirit of Jealousy (Numbers 5:14)

Sorrowful Spirit (1 Samuel 1:15)

Lustful Spirit (James 4:5)

Lazy Spirit (Romans 11:8)

Spirit of Infirmity (Luke 13:11)

These are *signs of the activity* of *familiar spirits*.

The Seven Spirits of God in the Bible:

The Bible does not tell us specifically who or what the seven spirits are, but one very strong indication that they are complete and full expressions of the same Holy Spirit, seems most likely to be what is described for us in Isaiah 11:2,

"The Spirit of the LORD will rest on him; the Spirit of wisdom and of understanding, the Spirit of counsel and of power, the Spirit of knowledge and of the fear of the LORD."

I believe this describes for us, *the seven spirits,* or *expressions* of God:

(1) Spirit of the LORD, (2) Spirit of Wisdom, (3) Spirit of Understanding, (4) Spirit of Counsel, (5) Spirit of Power, (6) Spirit of Knowledge, (7) Spirit of the Fear of the Lord.

I believe when the fullness of God's Holy Spirit is embraced and expressed through our own lives as Christians, we keep the door to familiar spirits closed, over our lives and the lives of those we love. The same applies for our churches. Learn to detect these trespassing spirits and instead of allowing them a place to operate in the church, be bold for Jesus and take a STAND! Drive them OUT by the power of God IN you, *in Jesus' Name.*

6

LOOSING UNGODLY SOUL TIES

The strongest form of soul tie is that of a sexual union. The Word of God states through sexual union, *the two become one.* It is a Godly union (Godly soul tie) that God intended for us all to have, and to be blessed by having.

That very union, and the two individuals becoming one in spirit, soul and body means exactly that: *everything of each of those two people individually, suddenly is inherited into the other. Absorbed into the other's spirit, soul, and body. The two become one.*

One of the two will dominate, even in the soul tie. You will notice one person's personality seem to take on the others, and will yield more to the other, but one will maintain dominance as in with all unions. One will be the one who yields to the others lead, as in all relationships. These, once two, now have a relationship. They give in to each other; yield to each other. They complement and encourage the other's life.

This same law of union unfortunately is activated as well in an *ungodly sexual union,* whether in adultery, fornication, molestation, rape, or incest. The very thing that God intended to work blessings through, the enemy has managed to warp and use for destructive purposes.

The ungodly soul ties we find ourselves bound to,

must be severed, and ultimately destroyed to continue in a healthy future filled with healthy relationships.

Ungodly Soul ties - Occur in relationships where generational curses are meshed. Co- dependency is another form of an unhealthy soul tie and is the enemies counterfeit to the place in our lives created for God to have.

People who we come to care for, we can also find ourselves loving more than we even love God. We say we love God, but we hold on to many compromising ways, and our lifestyles reflect it. We love God, *yes, in our heads with our intellect*, but our hearts (the core of our being) are far from Him if God is not heard in your speech or seen in your life. Good people do not have God in their lives simply because they are good people.

We are to love Him with all our heart, and mind and soul; but how can we if our heart, mind, and soul are fragmented and split over multiple devotions.

All ungodly soul ties leave you in pieces, fragmented. The power of the Blood of Jesus Christ severs ungodly soul ties, and without struggle.

When an ungodly soul tie is meshed with a familiar spirit you will have destruction, destructive behavior, destroyed hopes, dreams... *lives. It produces rebellion.*

Relationships that include sexual union, sexual activity outside of marriage are forms of ungodly soul ties. God's fullest blessing cannot truly be realized by relationships in this stage. Taking the next step, to assure the Lord's blessing would be to formerly unite, before God and man. Why? This is a public declaration of the two becoming one, with no more availability to others. The door to others is closed. Your relationship gets sealed with God's blessing, as you choose to unite His way, in covenant.

The Scriptures also describe the souls (the mind, will and emotions) of two men, that were knit or meshed: that of Jonathon and David (First Samuel 18). Important to note as well, that these two men are not described as having any sexual union between them, and yet God's word describes their friendship, their *oneness* as being *knit together,* and blessed of God.

I believe it to be a description of the love between two friends that ran as deep as the love between two brothers who would be bound by a **godly soul tie;** *one that reflected the love of God.* A devoted love and respect. Interesting how Satan has **perverted** the relationship of Jonathon and David **to appear** as **homosexual**. A mind that knows God, but a heart that is far from God will believe this way.

The devil knows God. Homosexuality is described as **vile affection**, in the Bible. It is described as **against nature** and the **natural** use or natural **function** of sexuality and sex. It also outlines the suffering in the body and personality, inevitable consequences, and penalty for this wrongdoing.

Romans 1:26-27 reads: *For this reason, God*

gave them over and abandoned them to vile affections and degrading passions. For their women exchanged their natural function for an unnatural and abnormal one, and the men also turned from natural relations with women and were set ablaze (burning out, consumed) with lust for one another – men committing shameful acts with men and suffering in their bodies and personalities the inevitable consequences and penalty of their wrongdoing and going astray, which was their fitting retribution.

A soul tie can be compared to the strength of an umbilical cord, between a mother and child, the lifeline. The mother and child are one, in a godly union, a godly soul tie. A Divine Connection between them that meshes, unites, binds, and ties them in spirit, soul and in body. At birth, when the umbilical cord is no longer needed, it is severed or cut from the mother.

This parallel is one I can identify with, when severing an *ungodly soul tie*, through prayer and intercession. In spiritual warfare, we take the power of the Blood of Jesus Christ and sever the ungodly soul ties that keep our loved ones bound, <u>and attached</u> to lives of sin, destruction, and defeat. Cut the cord, in Jesus' Name!

In warfare prayer, we sever what keeps the sin alive. The sinful source is identified and cut off.

People can be liberated by God's power. He also provides all the necessary means by which to maintain that liberty. The only thing that can yank a person back, comes through the power of choice **given to us by the Lord!** He leaves it up to us, to choose each day, how we will live that day. We have the power to choose to keep ourselves free from soul ties, that lead to pain and destruction. Soul ties, and connections with sin, sinfulness, and sinful people keep a person bound. You can always tell when a person is bound by their sin.

There is a constant inner struggle, as you war with something that <u>GOD IN YOU</u> KNOWS IS NOT RIGHT. When your KNOWER knows, you will remain in a state of unrest and agitation. You will always want to flee anywhere than where you are, but you know what is in you goes with you.

If it is sin, get it out!

Peace is only one choice away, in manners of inner turmoil stemming from sin. The power to destroy the ties that bind your soul, are within your power and your reach. You are one choice away, and the freedom to choose was given to you by God. Choose the path that leads to life!

7

STRONGHOLDS OF MINDSETS

Have you ever tried to get through to a person with lifesaving counsel, prayer, and advice only to see that you are trying *in vain? The more you try the worse they get.*

You can spend hours, for weeks and months at a time only to find at the end of it all, people do not follow those truths. Even if it is the Truth of God's word that will free them from the confusion, lack of blessings and suffering they are going through, you find a degree of *stubbornness and self-will* that goes beyond the norm; that is a strong hold in a person's mind that *is set.* **A stronghold of a mindset.**

A stronghold *of a mindset* is the same as when a person's way of believing is warped or twisted from what is good, or healthy for life. A way of believing; *an established set of attitudes.*

For example, you may know someone who lies so much, they believe what they are saying, regardless of how destructive it may be. They are *the only one who does not see* the destructiveness of the way the (1) attitude they hold, (2) what they believe, and (3) how it is dragging them through a life of pain, shame, and suffering, is stealing, killing, and destroying their life. In this case, the person's *own will* keeps them bound. We all have a choice.

All strongholds must yield to the Lordship of Jesus Christ. All strongholds obey the direction and order of God's authority, **when enforced.** That is a truth we are going to have to begin to realize, understand and grasp hold of. It is an authority that when enforced, brings forth results... sometimes quickly, *sometimes not so quickly.*

Another form of a stronghold of a mindset, comes through abuse. A victim can have a stronghold over their mind, in which the victim believes they will NEVER be free from their abuser. They hold to an attitude of despair and defeat, <u>even when a door presents itself for their freedom.</u>

When a person has been freed, liberated from a **force of control** working through another person, they often were not aware it was happening to such a great degree, and there is an initial shock.

I have witnessed individuals who have been freed through prayer from a mindset that was controlling, abusing, sabotaging, and even doused in witchcraft, suddenly be awakened, and a light seemingly rests on them. The hold on their mind has been broken. The light in their eyes is back.

It is so important to **_begin and to continue_** to help renew their lives, filling their lives with God's word, peace, love, and acceptance; compassion from fellow men and women of God... it is a *healing process and can take years to fully heal from.*

We forget the strain evil forces can take on a person's spirit, soul, **and** body. Healing is a process that takes time, with each day unfolding a new layer of healing and wholeness. We do well to continue helping in the healing process, by practicing patience and prayer for those afflicted, through to wholeness.

Our minds take on battle fatigue, from years of warring in prayer for long-lost loved ones. Unless we learn to roll the whole weight of those painful details, we will not have lasting relief. We must pull away and renew ourselves in the Lord, from the battles of the past, and for those challenges and battles ahead.

Renew your mind and your heart daily, and often several times throughout your day. Some days require more than others. The absolute one way to retain freedom from strongholds in the mind is to KEEP the mind fixed on the Lord and the things that pertain to our victory in Christ.

People, even Christians are guilty of repeatedly opening our minds to various beliefs that other people hold. We can be so weak-minded as to be continually formed and shaped by the strong beliefs of others.

This can only happen when we, as individuals do not really believe in anything. We are open to anything and everything, and never develop our own strong beliefs, for lack of true sanctification, true separation to God, in our lifestyles, or lifestyle choices.

When a person believes in something, conviction is developed. Conviction that causes us to hold fast and hold true regardless of what others around us do or say.

For some, our convictions vary depending on how we choose to respond to circumstances. Our convictions cause us to love God, be faithful to family and to attend church, live chaste, to give monetarily; but with a stronghold of a mindset, *in the back of your mind a frustration or anger that God has not come through for you fast enough, or somehow God has failed you; prayers have not been answered, financial woes, family dilemmas, married complexities and more, build up.*

By giving your mind over to strife and debate, you hold an argumentative countenance with others, because of conversations in the spirit of your mind, that have strengthened their hold.

Unresolved conflict can lead to a stronghold of the enemy, and the enemy will use it against you relentlessly. They have a weight of oppression about them, and are fatiguing and exhausting, even sickening. Our bodies take on the pain of the mind, and you can find yourself giving in to a drug or an alcohol *altar of depression and defeat.* If even for a moment, you surrendered to it.

Only the flesh, *and demons of the flesh* can be gratified by those weaknesses. Weakness gains ground and so does the enemy, for failure to fix *and re-fix* our thoughts in the Lord.

Isaiah 26:3, *"You keep him in perfect peace whose mind is stayed on you, because he trusts in you."*

Strongholds in the mind, come from fear and a lack of trust. God wants to resolve that issue for you. Unrest or restlessness over an issue, rob you of God's peace. He wants to resolve that issue for you, as well. God can and God will come through for you, hope in God. Reinforce and recommit your trust in a God who is able.

Seven Signs of Demon Activity/Influence

The order of this information is not necessarily the order the enemy uses in gaining influence over a person's life. The soul is the mind, will and emotions of a man, woman, or child. This is where the battle takes place, as you choose to live for God.

Many people have not settled in their minds and hearts that the Lord is not in a tug of war with the devil over anyone.

The battle was finished long ago, through the finished work of the cross and Christ crucified, died, and buried, then resurrected and ascended; soon to return. Those who belong to the Lord, will be with Him in the end. Those who do not, will not. We have the power to choose who we will serve and what we will reap: God or Satan, the blessing, or the curse.

The tug of war is between us individually, and ourselves. The part of us that chooses and decides is daily being bombarded with choices and decisions; some more self-gratifying, self-indulging and self-centered than what will get us into heaven. Paul speaks of this *tug-of-war* in the book of Romans. Will we or will we not, yield *our will* over to the *will of God,* each time we are challenged, lured, or tempted?

The soulish realm is the mind, will and emotions of man. These are areas of our life that are not instantly renewed at salvation. These are areas that must be (daily) turned over to God, to maintain the renewal of the Holy Spirit, by our faith.

Areas that must be (daily) introduced afresh to the boundaries and the blessings of God's word. Daily lifestyle changes and choices assure us of not **regressing,** or anything else that may harm our lives or the lives of others, ultimately.

1. **REGRESSION**: To revert to earlier behavior patterns; backwards; opposite of progression. When you stop making progress. When you find yourself losing ground you have gained or recovered in life.

This attack on a Christian individual will cause them to cease from flowing in the blessings, and in the gifts and talents God has given them, and literally cause him/her to move in the opposite direction from the perfect will of God for their life. It is what leads to backsliding; when a person who lives for God, *stops.*

Take Note:

Have you noticed yourself or someone you love, regressing in life?

I know Christians who make so much progress and gain so much ground, then regress to former behavior patterns, and former strongholds of mindsets like haughtiness, insecurity, vanity, low self-esteem, constant complaining and strife.

People who love God and are blessed in multiple ways, suddenly stop being grateful and instead with *nit-picky nonsense* use former fault-finding criticisms that are manifestations of how they see themselves. This is the spirit of regression.

You must stop yourself from self-sabotaging. *You* must cease from *your inner* anger because it will open the door to physical sickness and hurts the people around you. You already *sound* sick, by your double minded, fault finding speech. Get back where you belong in the Lord. You are not a victim of anything but your own vain imagination. God is good, and good to YOU!

Take the next step, even if it is a small one. It is still PROGRESS. A step at a time, a day at a time, is still PROGRESS. When you make *Pro*gress, you have stopped to *Re*gress. Progression is the opposite of regression.

Take steps toward God. This is what it means to submit to God, and to His leading. When you take this bold step, you make Jesus glad and the devil mad, stopping regression in its tracks.

2. **REPRESSION**: Restrain, squeeze; preventing the natural expression of yourself or another person. For one person to repress another, or for someone else to repress you are both *not of God*, and unhealthy. Eventually the body itself, begins to wear down, and feel worn out. We can be repressive to ourselves. Repression is a mental process by which thoughts and memories that cause anxiety, are ignored.

This behavior causes and disables an individual

from freely expressing themselves through healthy emotions, and thoughts.

I have known churches that will forcefully stop an individual who is quietly worshipping the Lord on bended knee, at the Altar! That is a Stronghold of Repression in a church that quenches and grieves the Holy Spirit, Who is ministering to the life of a worshipper expressing gratitude.

Homes can also be repressive when the atmosphere is miserable and there is no joy.

I do not remember having a repressive childhood, so maybe that is why I did not recognize it when I married young and ended up abused and divorced.

What began as repression ended in a degree of domestic violence that nearly killed me, my five-month-old daughter *and unborn baby.* I was two months pregnant by my repressive, abusive, alcoholic, drug addict, **out-of-the-will-of-God,** husband.

Repression is a devil of control.

3. **SUPPRESSION**: To press under, keep back; to exclude or lessen the importance of your own desires or feelings. To keep yourself under a degree of control that inhibits who you are when whole. It is the act of deliberately keeping something from happening.

A person **who holds their own** feelings or *hides* their **own true desires or feelings** is a suppressed person. Many people who suppress themselves can also cause people they meet, to suppress their own thoughts, opinions, ideas, or other healthy expressions of life, and suffer physically because of it.

There are grown adult men who were not allowed to cry as a child, because of an upbringing that included the teaching that *'boys don't cry'*. As adults those suppressed emotions have been carried into relationships that suffer, because of an ungodly, unhealthy upbringing in a suppressed environment.

God through His Word reveals His own great exhuberation and openness of desires and feelings. His own *likes, dislikes,* etc. Think about that for a good moment...

Have you been holding back who you really are? Have you been hiding?

Many overly shy and bashful people have suppressed themselves often for fear of ridicule or perceived ridicule. For fear of rejection, many people will hold back from healthy expressions that identify them in Christ.

Others have learned to keep to themselves where upbringing did not allow you freedom of expression. For example, some childhood upbringings included sitting still and being quiet: *children were to be seen and not heard. Remember those days?* It led right to suppression.

Forcing a child ***not to cry***, after you spanked the near life out of them forms suppression. **The**

natural thing for a child to do that has been physically pained from physical discipline is to cry. *And cry very loud.* **Forceful stopping** of that **naturally born instinct** *is suppressive.*

4. **DEPRESSION**: The continual hold of a downcast countenance, lowliness and gloom, despair and dejection, emotional disconnection; *sadness beyond what is a normal, healthy grief is a sign of depression in its early stages.*

Decrease in strength, desire, or activity; lack of self-motivation, and multiple, unfinished projects are a sign of depression. Apathy and indifference are also subtle, vague traces of this sickness. This is a *soulish*, emotional condition which can become neurotic or even psychotic, and is often characterized by the multiplied, overwhelming feelings and bombardments of continual hopelessness, dejection, insufficiency, as well as inadequacy. A belief or feeling that *"it's never enough, it's never good enough, it will never change..."* are clues of depression.

I find it humorous when people make chide, criticizing and insensitive remarks concerning depression, and REFUSE to admit or recognize *THEY THEMSELVES* are depressed. Denial is the first give away.

Depression is a *creeper.* It is a *naturally* dormant spirit that likes to retreat and play *possum* to avoid detection. The Holy Spirit **always** detects this and all spirits that are not of God.

Are *you depressed? How do you know?*

Major Depression is defined as including loss of interest in activities that were once interesting or enjoyable. The activities affected include sex, food, and people. With a loss of appetite comes weight fluxuations, loss of emotional expression *(flat affect)*, and persistent sadness.

Other signs are anxious or empty mood, feelings of hopelessness, pessimism, guilt, worthlessness or helplessness, social withdrawal, unusual fatigue, low energy level, a feeling of being slowed down. Sleep disturbance with insomnia, early morning awakening, or oversleeping, trouble concentrating, remembering, or making decisions, unusual restlessness, or irritability, also plague the person who is assaulted by depression. *Persistent* physical problems such as headaches, digestive disorders or chronic pain that does not respond to treatment, thoughts of death or suicide or suicidal attempts. Alcohol or drug use or abuse may also signal depression and are often included as forms of self-medication.

Powerful, disabling moments, episodes and sometimes seasons of major depression can occur in a person's life, and be triggered unexpectedly, *or not triggered at all.*

50% of Ministers and Pastors end in divorce; 70% are depressed.

Ministers includes people in Helps, lay ministry and volunteers.

Evidence of a complete broken spirit is found in the satanic control of depression's force. The continued pressure against a person's spirit until that spirit is crushed is Satan's objective.

Depression is a destructive force and often opens the door wide to sickness and disease. Many times, the state of sadness a person is in is so great there can be no real expression of that sadness; almost as if the individual has "shutdown". An emotional disconnection with the most important people in their lives, begins to be expressed through the person being held by depression. They start to *die, to deteriorate* from the inside out like a cancer.

Depression is an extremely violent and vicious demonic force whose goal is self-destruction and premature death.

People who suffer depression, do not always suffer it for long bouts at a time. These bouts with depression *come and go,* some longer and harder than others depending on the circumstances that surround, and often *trigger* depression. I often compare depression like a wave of the sea. Some waves are harder than others, but as soon as they hit, they begin to dispel their strength; *but they hit hard,* nonetheless, and sometimes there was no *trigger*.

People who have gained victory over depression are sensitive to many other subtle maneuvers the enemy works, in keeping the spirit of depression strong in a person who is bound.

These are people who have formed, *like radar, an* ability to seek and find others who remain bound and depressed, *and through experiencing* God's faithfulness to His Word, are setting these people free. Through recognition of demonic forces when they are actively present, and by *authoritative* removal of them, people who have nearly been destroyed by the devil of depression, are being liberated from their stronghold, **and not with medication!**

Victorious people, who through right relationship with God, have demonstrated the liberating power of God, and defeated the effects of depression without prescription medication or other unhealthy forms of **self**-*medicating*.

The devil of depression cannot hold on to a person who resists by *authoritative use* of the power of the Blood of Jesus Christ, who resists by the power of God's faithful promises: **His Word.**

Submission to God is the power behind your resistance. It is the only way the devil in his many forms, flees and loosens God's people.

5. **OPPRESSION**: Pressure to crush, smother, or overpower; to overwhelm, harass, ravish, or rape.

This attack is one of the more extremes in cruelty. Weights of unbearable pressure are loaded on the life of a person targeted with this attack, **one load at a time.**

Often it is through many, multiple attacks at once that the enemy arrays his onslaught in a desperate attempt to break and overpower his target: you.

Oppression comes from outer elements, or situations of pressure that are restraining, limiting, and binding. A person in authority who is unfair and cruel, who prevents another person's opportunities, or prevents them of emotional expression, *is an oppressor.*

Oppression is a heavy harassing force; agitating and constant. One sign of oppression is a mind full of thoughts with no end. Not being able to "think things through" without outer, constant interruptions and demands from others. Heavy demands and expectations from others, and over-the-top criticisms and gestures working through others, as if in displeasure with you is a sign you are suffering some oppression.

The mind becomes fixed on expectations, shortcomings, fear of failure, etc. The body begins to respond to the overload of thoughts, and before you know it there is physical pain somewhere; *everywhere.* Exhaustion kicks in, and teams up with Fatigue, I call *battle fatigue.*

You are in a critical place. Your first and most immediate need is Strength, Peace... and all roads lead to Jesus! *Can you recall an oppressive situation you have observed in the past?*

6. OBSESSION: To besiege, to haunt (as by an evil spirit); to be fixed or focused on a single *thought, person, or object* to an unreasonable degree, is obsession. Obsession is ruled by lust and perversion.

This force of evil requires true fasting to free the person controlled by obsession, for it is at this stage that the individual has absolutely no control of their own thoughts, will or emotions; their mind has been totally given over to the object of their obsession and it literally *drives their every action, dominates their every sense of reason; rules their every mood and emotion.*

The person who suffers an ungodly obsession is formed by a different, more overpowering personality.

All perspective is gone; everything about this person is out of touch with all that surrounds him/her. They are ruled and driven by the most unreasonable thoughts, having begun to believe those thoughts are the reality.

Prodigal children are **ruled by obsession**. It begins with the lust of the flesh, the lust of the eyes and the pride of life, the fixation of self-gratification.

This spirit of obsession is dominated by a spirit of antichrist. It is its own god. The pursuit for self-gratification, self-adoration, self-gain, and empowerment at all costs.

One example of an individual who is obsessed by an evil force of the demonic, is a loved one who is suddenly *borderless*. A loved one who is consumed in their thoughts, hardened in their heart and abusive in their speech. Disloyal and disrespectful of sound reasoning and wise instruction, these are people who have turned their back on everything pertaining to God, only choosing to keep God on the backburner *"in case things go wrong"*.

As if God were a personal puppet charm we can carry around in our pocket and pull out and chant to when we need Him.

These are people who were raised to know God and the things that pertain to righteous living, in a world and society of unrighteousness. These are often former children of God, who have made themselves to be children of wrath.

Sudden reckless living is a sign of obsession. Sudden careless, dangerous, and defiant living is a sign of an unruly obsessive person who is on the FAST TRACK to disaster.

Your prayers as an Intercessor before the Lord keeps and preserves these loved ones. Notice, there is a difference between an Intercessor and a prayer-partner. Intercessor is based on the Scriptures, while prayer-partner is a loose term used to describe people who pray in agreement, over a situation. Intercessors pray all the way through to the result.

Intercessors do not have to know all the details of a situation or a person. Intercessors do not have to *pray about it*. Intercessors never *clock out*, but have a developed lifestyle of infused, saturated conversation with the Father, maintaining the practicing of God's presence.

We need to bring in the Intercessors when engaging in spiritual warfare for the deliverance of a loved one bound by Satan. Intercessors have the *fine tuning* of the Holy Spirit, and the *endurance* to pray loved ones **all the way through**, to victory in Christ.

If you are a prayer partner, ***shift gears.*** Step up to the anointing of an Intercessor and truly experience ***Moves of God***, like never. Intercessors set captives, free.

7. POSSESSION: To inhabit, occupy, control; to own. To hold as a property, dominate, actuate, or rule another person by extraneous force against his/her will. *Demon possession is the occupying of one's soul by demon presence... Christians, Holy Spirit filled, cannot be occupied by the devil and by God simultaneously. The word possessed, means "owned". A Christian CAN BE* <u>*influenced by demons*</u> *when they open the door to sin and compromise their convictions.*

This stage has the individual absolutely under the control and dominion of Satan. Their voice changes upon manifestation; they cannot look in the eye (the window of the soul) of a Spirit filled Christian. Matt 6:22-23.

The eyes of the demon possessed person reflect a black demonic glare. The way this person walks and dresses changes. They become very unclean;

demon possession usually begins through association with another person who is also demon possessed.

As recently as four or so years ago, my husband and I opened our home to help two people, a father, and a son.

Our home not only serves as parsonage for us, but also has provided shelter and basic needs for so many people, families, single parents, single adults, and throw-away teenagers who find themselves homeless. It was not much of a thought, to provide help to these two individuals, temporarily.

One early evening while preparing dinner, in the middle of a conversation the father asked me a question, which had its answer in the Lord. It was a question about the real-ness of God. This is the same as questioning God's existence or all-powerful authority.

Alerted in my spirit by the question, I proceeded to cut onions and while answering, looked up at him only to see Satan glaring back at me through his eyes. You KNOW the satanic when you see it. The devil will use the kindness of your heart, to gain entry to your life and home.

He had jumped up on my kitchen counter and crouching, glared at me with the blackest, emptiest, most evil eyes, and with a grin on his face, said, *"how do you know?"*

Immediately the Spirit of the Lord said, "Anti-Christ...occult...Satanist."

Within hours this man had created more turmoil, spun more lies and caused more division, anger and pain, even abusing his son in front of me. His son was a young adult but lost and undone without God. He was a wanderer and had been homeless for years when we brought him into our home. He was a great kid and no troublemaker in any way. A cool kid. This child was present when his mother overdosed on hard drugs, when he was young enough to remember finding her.

In no time, the man was on a one-way ride by bus, to Central Texas. Get the devil and his own, out of your house. *Kind heart or not* get the devil out in Jesus' Name and do not let him back in!

STRONGMEN/STRONGHOLDS
Characteristics and Signs of Demon Activity

*Or how can a person go into a **strongman's house** and carry off his goods (everything he owns) without **first binding the strong man?** Then indeed he may plunder his house.*
Matthew 12:29

*For the weapons of our warfare are not physical, but they are mighty before God for the pulling down, overthrow and destruction of **strongholds**.*
2 Cor. 10:4

*The seventy returned with joy saying, Lord, even the **demons are subject to us in your name**! And He said to them, I saw Satan falling like lightening from heaven. Behold! I have given you authority and power to trample upon serpents and scorpions, and (physical and mental strength and ability) **over all the power that the enemy possesses;** and nothing shall in any way harm you.* **Luke10:17**

One very important detail to **Effective Prayer** that I learned early in my Christian life was in dealing with the source of the problem *in prayer,* getting to *the root* of the issue. We learned early on, not to spend important times of intercession and *warfare-prayer* addressing the manifestations of the enemy, such as anger or envy. The <u>source of the problem</u>, where all the strength for those *shows-of-strength*, was **Jealousy.**

With simple fine tuning in my prayer life, the tide of the battle turned. Instead of rebuking and coming against the aches and pain in my body, I learned to bind the strongman of Infirmity, and loose the healing power of God over and through me, in Jesus' Name. I learned what was required to have that ability demonstrated in my life as a Christian.

I dove in, so to speak, in building my relationship with God the Father, God the Son and God the Holy Spirit as shown and directed to us in the Bible.

It changed my life. Instead of resisting *the symptoms of depression*, I learned to bind and rebuke the stronghold of Heaviness; and I saw change!

The Lord has given us **all that we will need** to *expel the evil* that attaches itself to our loved ones, to our lives. Those root causes to our sickness and disease, to bondage and our freedom from it is found in the strongmen/strongholds of the devil. ***What you bind on earth, is bound in heaven; what you loose on earth is loosed in heaven.*** Bind the evil and loose the Good. Take charge over your prayer life and ask the Lord to baptize you in His power and ability to exercise your faith and authority over the devil. God is with you!

STRONGMAN: Jealousy
(Numbers 5:14-30)
Manifestations of demons are:
Insecurity, rage (Proverbs 6:34), revenge, murder
(Gen 4), competitive jealousy, false accuser,
anger, restlessness, suspicion, envy, covetous,
competitive, self-admirer/comparer

STRONGMAN: Familiar Spirits
(1 Sam. 28:7)
Manifestations of demons are:
Astrology, horoscope, fortune telling,
false prophets, psychics, occult, new age,
death, surfacing old *habits* and
generational curses that have once broken,
consulter of demons, divination.

It is in the church! As a believer, we are born **again** under the sign of the Cross! What is a Christians obsession with their astrological *sign?* This is *only one* example of a weak, unguarded mind.

STRONGMAN: Perversion
(to twist or corrupt the truth) (Isaiah 19:14)
Manifestation of demons are:
Hate God (Proverbs 14:2); have a wounded spirit
(Proverbs 15:4), lust (Proverbs 23:33), will bring
error, doctrinal error, lovers of self, drunkenness,
confusion, uncleanness, disrespectful of all forms
of authority and boundaries, unruly. Distracted
and distracting, seeking attention for self. Pride.

STRONGMAN: Heaviness
(Isaiah 61:3)
Manifestations of demons are:
Unnatural grief, self-pity, rejection, lowliness, gluttony, despair, hopelessness, gloomy, downcast, sorrowful, bitter, complaining (1 Sam 1:15-16), depression, brokenness, devastation, shame. sense of inadequacy, incompleteness, exhaustion, dissatisfaction with everything around them, isolation. Social and emotional disconnection, loneliness.

STRONGMAN: Whoredom
(Hosea 4:12-19)
Manifestations of demons are:
Idol worship, idolatry, love of the world and love of money, fellowship with unbelievers, fornication, wanderers, prostitution (also read Ezekiel 16:28), unfaithful, stubborn, ruin, spirit of the world, new age. Avoids the subject and is very uncomfortable around the subject of the Blood of Jesus Christ, the cross, and the Holy Spirit. Backsliders.

STRONGMAN: Infirmity
(Luke 13:11-13)
Manifestation of the demons are:
All physical, mental, emotional sickness, weakness of spirit, soul (will, emotions and mind), and of body, downcast, spiritual blindness, deafness to God's will. All disease is ruled by Infirmity. All infirmity is weakness.

Weak-minded people are ruled by infirmity;

those who cannot control their thoughts, are weak in their mind, not able to resist unclean, impure, and often vile thoughts and images.

Weak natured people are ruled by Infirmity; those bound by unnatural expressions of affection, or other traits that are held by all things holy, or as pure and righteous. A failing or defect in a person's character is infirmity, *by definition.*

Spiritually dwarfed people are ruled by Infirmity; those who do not strengthen or increase in their faith in God. Lack of strength is a sign of Infirmity; lack of strength *in our faith* is proven by a lack of growth in our personal walk with God. God's word instructs us to, **"increase in our faith",** which is to "grow strong in our faith."

Wherever you find sickness and weakness, lack or deficiency, illness, or ***dis-ease*** as well as disease, you will find a dominant spirit of Infirmity.

Infirmity is **ruled** by doubt, fear, and bondage. A triple cord held together by lies. God's overcoming power breaks the hold of *devils of lies, devils of doubt and devils of fear* in the mighty Name of Jesus Christ. By His Blood, by His truth entering us, filtering out the debris of deadly fear and unbelief we CHOOSE LIFE!

And with LONG LIFE He satisfies us and shows us His salvation! (Psalm 91:16)

I shall not die but live and shall declare the works and of the Lord. (Psalm 118:17)

STRONGMAN: Deaf and Dumb
(Mark 9:17-25)
Manifestations of demons are:
This spirit rules over suicide, insanity, seizures, motionless, epilepsy, lunatic, madness, roaming and unclean spirit (also read Matthew 17:15).

STRONGMAN: Antichrist
(1 John 4:3-6)
Manifestations of demons are:
Legalism, speaking against Gifts of the Holy Spirit, substitutes everything for the Blood of Jesus, blasphemy, controlling spirit, witchcraft, dominating, attack your testimony, disturb church services; avoids the Blood of Jesus, will not even talk about it; are restless around the subject of the Blood of Jesus Christ; non-confession of Christ.

STRONGMAM: Fear
(Mark 5:36, 2 Tim 1:7)
Manifestations of demons are:
Doubt, nightmares, worry, unbelief, phobia, panic, torment, terror, sense of danger, timidity, inferiority, inadequate (also read Hebrews 12:21; Rev 2:10), anxiety, powerless.

STRONGMAN: Pride
(Isaiah 16:6, Psalm 35:16, 2 Chr. 30:7-9)
Manifestations of demons are:
Haughtiness, conceit, false boasting on self, hypocrite, scornful, mockery, stubbornness, witchcraft, gossip, wrath, arrogance, controlling, self-righteous, denial; demeaning of others. looking down on others. Lies.

STRONGMAN: Lying Spirit
(2 Chr. 18:20)
Manifestations of demons are:
False prophecy, seduction, trickery and manipulation. (also Read 1 King 22:21-23)

STRONGMAN: Bondage
(Romans 8:15)
Manifestations of demons are:
Cannot call upon God or refer to Him as Father. Anguish, bitterness, addiction (all types), spiritual blindness, cannot hear the voice of the Holy Spirit.

STRONGMAN: Error
(1 John 4:6)
Manifestations of demons are:
Loveless, indifference, find fault, twist Scriptures, avoids or becomes aggressive over the subject of the Holy Spirit, Scriptures, or the Blood of Jesus. Contrary and contradicting use of Scripture.

STRONGMAN: Seduction
(1 Timothy 4:1-3)
Manifestations of demons are:
False doctrine, liars, delusion, and hypocrisy.
seared conscience. Lust and perversion work
closely with this spirit. Enticing and luring,
mesmerizing and captivating others through lies,
manipulation and flattery. Webs of deception
called vanity keep this stronghold, ***strong***.

STRONGMAN: Deep Sleep
(Isaiah 29:10-13)
Manifestations of demons are:
Spiritual blindness, no vision, no understanding,
no motivation. Cannot perceive the voice of the
Lord or the timing of God and therefore resist the
move of the Holy Spirit for a lack of clarity and
discernment; always need an *awakening*, a
"revival" but never maintain the awakening
or the reviving. Spiritual sluggard.

STRONGMAN: Disobedience
(Eph. 2:2-5)
Manifestations of demons are:
Lies, worldly, mockery, lust, corruption, unclean,
spiritually dead, no fellowship with Christ,
witchcraft, rebellion, unbelief, at war with
God's purpose, children of wrath.

STRONGMAN: Divination
(Acts 16:16-21)
Manifestations of demons are:
Demon possession, witchcraft, sorcery,
fortunetelling, psychic, to *glorify* man over God,
annoying, lies, superstitions and traditions of
man are a tool of this spirit.

STRONGMAN: Unclean Spirit
(Zechariah 13:2-6, Matt. 12:43,
Matt. 15:18-20, Luke 11:24, Mark 5:8-13)
Manifestations of demons are:
False prophecy, lies, shameful, deception, denial,
wounded, betrayal, self-abusive, self-destructive,
lazy, roamers, restless, lost, familiar spirit,
turmoil, murder, adultery, sexual vice, theft,
false witness, slander, irreverent speech, suicide,
legion, multiple personality.

STRONGMAN: Spirit of the World
(Isaiah 19:3, 1 Corinthians 2:12-14)
Manifestations of demons are:
Devotion to things celebrated by the world of
which God has no part. Open idolatry, sorcery,
familiar spirits, new age, cursed, humanism and
the exaltation of human power as a superpower
without God. Self-adoration, self-exaltation,
lust, perversion, uncleanness, lewd,
lascivious, dirty, smutty, indecent.

STRONGMAN: Evil Spirit
(1 Sam 16:14-23, 18:10-30)
Manifestations of demons are:
Torment, trouble, ill, irritating and mischievously
deceptive; tiredness, exhaustion, fatigued,
unclean and lazy, ravenous, madness, anger
of a murdering degree, hateful, fearful of
anointing, manipulating, instigating,
covetous, jealousy; i**mp-ish.**

ORDER OF DELIVERANCE

Basically, on the order of deliverance, one should know that there is a real deception in the idea that an individual must *first be full of the Word of God* to prove deliverance from demon influence, or demon possession.

Also, another deception is that only certain individuals are *"gifted"* to take a demon oppressed or possessed individual through deliverance. The key is your Salvation. Do you belong to Jesus Christ, to begin with? Have you received the Holy Ghost since you have believed?

Acts 19:2, He said to them, "Did you receive the Holy Spirit when you believed?" (in the Lord Jesus Christ). And they said to him, "No, we have not even heard whether there is a Holy Spirit."

To also have an established relationship with the Lord, and remain sensitive to the Holy Ghost, prayed up and stirred up in the gifts that God has endowed you with, is where the power is found. Knowing that above all, *one of the signs* of a believer is the ability to cast out devils, cleanse the lepers, raise the dead, heal the sick and so forth as found in the Book of Mark 16:17.

Acts 19 is vital. Multitudes are erroneously engaging in bouts of spiritual warfare, vainly attempting to cast out devils, with no true binding relationship, with the Lord.

It is a form of witchcraft.
It is a strange fire to God.

True, **Effective Spiritual Warfare** is only attainable by and through the three-fold cord of Christ: His Name, His Blood, His Presence; it is the Power of God, revealed and demonstrated, *giving all* honor and glory to God.

There are not enough people **digging deep** into the Word of God; **digging deep** to ensure the founded stability of our relationship with the Lord is **established**. We fall short in this and fail to tap into the power made available to us, for all our *busy-ness.*

We are just plain and simple **too busy, too distracted**, and too un-devoted of our time and attention, as required for the battle. Engaging in spiritual warfare, intercession, prophetic ministry, or the preaching of His Word **with little to no true set-apart time** with God, is an open door to disaster, and invites spiritual attacks.

Many Christians are engaged in levels of spiritual warfare and eager, *pre-maturely,* to operate in the gifts of the Holy Spirit yet are lacking in being fully disciplined in *time alone* with God. Then there are those, pastors included, who can have quality time with the Lord, and instead busy themselves with non- sense. You will know them by the lack of anointing and power in the church. The church of Jesus Christ is to demonstrate to unbelievers, the power of God. Too many of God's churches are powerless. No one is being set free. People are leaving the same way they came in.

There is no formula to follow, for deliverance. But you must follow the leading of the Holy Ghost that comes from an *established* *relationship* with the Lord. You must be in upright relationship with the Father to be able to effectively minister deliverance to a person in bondage, to people who are suffering evil assignments.

Know that when the Holy Spirit comes upon you to set a captive person free, there is no time to waste in trying to find out whether the person needing liberty has met certain criteria, or where they are in their lives, or if they attend church and who is their pastor... *obviously,* they need BREAKTHROUGH, so *break them through* to a new life in Christ! The anointing of God's presence comes upon you to set people free.

You must act on the anointing God is providing for that given circumstance; act speedily and *with the authority* that God has invested in you. It is in you for a reason greater than yourself; it is in you to free others. Delay can open a door to a missed opportunity to demonstrate the liberating power of God's word in a person's life.

I say speedily and without delay, for the simple reason that often there are only windows of opportunity, when the Presence of the Lord is the strongest, and that is when you see results.

Timing is everything.

People need **the power of God that FREES!**

We need a demonstration of the Holy Spirit, not sermon series and sermonettes.

We need a move of God. We need a move of the Holy Ghost, more and more, as Jesus walks among us, to touch, heal and liberate!

Jesus came for the sick. The finished work of the cross made the way possible for us all to have the opportunity for Divine Healing.

The truth that Jesus came for the sick, *did not heal the sick.* The truth imparted, **and received as truth,** brings forth the Divine Healing of God for our lives, to be realized and experienced, personally.

After the Ascension of Jesus, there were still a whole lot of people left here, who had not received the truth of what was made available by the victory of Christ on the cross. People who **still do not know**, there is a way to fight back, and WIN! We have a whole lot of work to do, in imparting those truths, so the benefits of the cross can be realized, by people, personally.

EMBLEMS and SIGNS

OF DEMON/OCCULT POWER

Even as God has symbols of His power and His holiness (oil, tabernacle, Shekinah glory, utensils, etc.), so Satan also has symbols of his wickedness. Here is a short list of some, and *yes there are many.*

A simple study of signs and symbols helps in identifying areas of entry and occupation.

Good luck charms, four leaf clovers, rabbit's foot, or other good "luck" tokens, are regularly used by witches and fortune tellers. Dolls or puppets made in other countries are often used in voodoo or witchcraft and are made in the guise of children's toys. Statues of fire gods, elephant statues or images such as these are worshipped in other countries as *gods,* and **should not** be found in homes of Christians, especially.

Characters: Many cartoon characters, troll dolls and merchandise (symbolic of, and often resembling literal demons), unicorns, crystals, prisms, and rainbows are all used in the Cult religion of New Age and some have been adopted to represent a Homosexual lifestyle.

You may notice a rise in nightmares and *"invisible friends",* among young children and pre-teens after continual viewing of many types of television programs.

These are programs designed ***subliminally*** to **desensitize our children**, by slowly introducing them **repeatedly** to images, situations, demonic and evil spirits and beliefs, and accepted lifestyles such as use of magic, charms, and chants to obtain and release power.

Subliminal messages and back-masking *were never fully done away with.* These deviant forms of mind filtration, formation and mind control are still used today, except that those responsible have become a bit more clever and subtle in their use.

FAMILIAR-*ity* with Ouija boards and many role play games, even music by secular artists, because many of today's secular artists are idolized, and many worship false gods themselves, **openly.** Jewelry of serpents, Ankh jewelry, jewelry, or clothing of anything portraying death and skulls. Chinese writing that cannot be translated by you should not be given a place in your home as many have sayings that are a curse and bondage over the home to foreign tradition, and you unknowingly give it a place in your home, unaware.

Jewelry, trinkets, and collectibles from foreign countries should be scrutinized closely. I say this not to bring a sense of paranoia upon you, but to keep you on your guard. Many have purchased small items from countries they visit and these items have been dedicated to gods and even to demons, and made in honor of those gods, by the individuals who craft them. Many "Christian" jewelry of crosses, and double crosses are used in Latin American religious cult ceremonies.

Incense is used by witches and sorcerers in

religious ceremonies to offer up their petitions to Satan, during their prayer and fasting rituals; *personally,* I no longer allow incense in my home, for that reason. There are other ways to create a nice scent in our homes.

Movies or literature on subjects of lust and sexual perversion, violence, and degrading of others, hate and bloodshed, should not be allowed in the home. The more we see them, the more **insensitive** we become to lust, to sexual perversion, to violence or revenge, and to the thoughts and language that go along with it. The eye is the window to the soul. The gateway to the mind, will and emotions. Get enough cussing coming through your television and it will not be long before everyone in the house is slipping cuss. Have you heard of transferring spirits? This is one way by which they transfer; by which they filter into our homes.

With literature, the same applies. Look at pornography even ONE TIME and the image is locked before your eyes, until the Blood of Jesus frees you. People go from one look to years of bondage to *sexual comparisons and dissatisfactions.* Like all other addictions, you are left empty and without, with **lifelong harmful** effects. All from just one look.

Do these things, *lust, and sexual perversions*, strengthen your life, your relationships, or glorify God in any way? Any of these objects or items that are in your home should not only be removed but they should be burned, shattered, or destroyed so they do not end up in someone else's home, thus opening their homes and lives to devilish troubles.

I am telling you I have burned books from my days of practicing witchcraft, *before I gave my life over to the Lordship of Jesus Christ.* Books that **refused to burn!**

Get it out of your house; all **of it.** I have burned video tapes and jewelry **that refused to burn,** so drenched and dedicated to the evil that was its source. Too often, we take lightly the things that are *right before our eyes,* not realizing it is through those very eyes, **that the light or darkness** of our soul, is determined.

The eye is the window, the lamp of the soul.
Through the eye, the soul is filled with light,
unless that light is darkness.

Matthew 6:22 states, *'The eye is the lamp of the body; so, then if your eye is clear, your whole body will be full of light. (V. 23) "but if your eye is bad, your whole body will be full of darkness. If then the light that is in you is darkness, how great is the darkness.*

The Word of God in 2 Timothy 2:20, 21 speaks of utensils or vessels in our earthly home which are of gold and silver (honorable use) and some that are of wood and earthenware (ignoble use); it also signifies in the spirit the same regarding our body *(the vessel of the Lord).*

You should study these Scriptures and ask the Holy Spirit *to teach you* and reveal areas in your home as well as your body that stand to be cleansed and set apart for His noble purposes. *When was the last time you did some spiritual housecleaning?*

Well, that is too long!

In the world of demons and witchcraft, the individuals who practice such vile acts will also dedicate their home and body to the satanic and set these apart for the ignoble use of satan.

What we allow in our homes makes all the difference in the world; *ignorance (lack of knowledge) is not excusable.* We have the tools by which to become knowledgeable and need only act upon what we have learned to be true.

I know a woman who began to see a sudden change in behavior with her husband, as if he were being unfaithful. She spent quite a bit of time staying particularly aware of his coming and going, only to find he was not going anywhere for any real length of time; she could not put her finger on it, *but she knew something was wrong.*

Before long, the mood in the home changed. His mood toward her changed, and he became more withdrawn, and agitated by her. To make a long story short, he had developed a pornographic habit that had increased to such a degree, he was now an active voyeur.

Voyeurism is the practice of obtaining sexual gratification by looking at sexual objects or acts, especially secretively. This man had allowed his mind to fixate on objects other than his wife...

he had gone so far as to clip and paste photos of the faces of the women in their family, over pornographic photos in magazines.

She did not like his love of pornographic material in the house but *could never do anything about it.* To avoid the strife and the argument that came along with voicing her dissatisfaction of this material in her home and around her children, she stopped saying anything and suppressed her feelings.

The **unchecked, uncontrolled, and unclean** thoughts of this man's *mind, heart and life* has destroyed his marriage, his reputation, and his family. He was arrested videotaping women in a Walmart parking lot.

Give NO PLACE to devils of pornography, lust, and perversion. Get it out of your home, in the Name of Jesus. Get it out from the secret places, and God will bless your home, your family, and *YES! YOUR MARRIAGE,* in Jesus Name.

It is Time to Clean House!

It is Time to Live for God! It is Time to Experience a Life in Christ, Fully Dedicated, and Set-Apart!

If you are ever going to experience a truly clean, set apart, sanctified, and dedicated to God, home, it is going to be after **Spiritual Housecleaning.** Get the devils out! Give no place, the Word of God states, to the devil (Ephesians 4:27), no foothold! Make no room for the flesh, either. In Romans 13:14, the Word of God instructs us to "put on Christ and make no provision for the flesh" or for its gratification. It pays to be clothed in the Lord!

Demons love carnal Christians.

The International Standard Version of the Word of God states it this way: *"do not give the devil an opportunity or place to work"*. That includes, nothing to work with!

Your home should reflect and resemble a place where peace is found. Make room, create a place where the peace of God, the presence of God can work, and you will see the tide of the battle turn for you.

The angels of the Lord surround those who do. Our homes and the rooms in our homes should be signs of good, peaceful, and free from constant turmoil and strife. Often, the home is divided with some rooms reserved for unclean, rebellious, defiant, impish spirits that work through our young one, teenagers and even many of today's young adults!

Spirits clash! The spirit of God in you, and the spirit of the world working through today's young people are warring for territory; for authority and even for respect not earned.

Instead of throwing out your loved one, get strong in the Lord and get the devil out!

God gives us wisdom, power, and strength. He gives us the ability to love our loved ones through to deliverance for the hold of the devil.

8

GET DELIVERED, STAY DELIVERED

I will never the day, the place, and the moment I was delivered from years of witchcraft, anger and a sickness that was leading me to death.

My sinful life *deserved* the sentence I was suffering. I had lived a life full of sin. I needed a new life! I needed a life that erased the sin and the stain of it all, once and for all.

I needed deliverance!

Demons had run me for such a long time, and I did not even know it. I am not talking about blaming the devil for everything I have ever done wrong; I am referring to the evil influences and evil interruptions that were key to my bondage. Devils that kept me bound, by ignorance.

Opportunity for life change is available to each person, ever born on the face of the earth. Through what we have obtained, if only utilized and put into action, we are assured of the delivering, freeing power of Jesus Christ.

I often, and repeatedly hear people give up and give in to how they were born. We were all born in iniquity and sin. We are all sinners, saved only by His grace.

Psalm 51:5 states, '*Behold I was brought forth in*

iniquity, and in sin my mother conceived me.

Once you recognize that you are in sin, that you are a sinner and were born that way, you have a choice to make. You **can** be born again! No religion can guarantee this Truth. Only your relationship with Christ can make that happen.

Psalm 51:5 continues with God desiring us to be truthful with ourselves. In our innermost being, for it is in that place of absolute honesty, truthfulness, and admission that He makes His wisdom known... we will know what to do, because of truth in our inmost heart.

The born-again experience is not something that happens because you go to church, or because you pray when things are bad, nor is it what you know about God.

The born-again experience is not something we are automatically entitled to, because our parents know God or because you are a good person. To be born again, does not happen without evidence of the born-again experience.

The born-again experience is the fire of God's Holy Spirit that KEEPS you in the way of the Lord. It is the power to KEEP you from giving in to carnal desires, lustful temptations, compromise and ungodly soul-*ish* bonds.

You MUST be Born-Again!

It takes the Holy Spirit of God to deliver you from evil, and it is the Holy Spirit of God that **equips and empowers you** to *MAINTAIN* your deliverance.

Get delivered and stay delivered!

Everything to FREE you from bondage, enters you at Salvation. The Salvation experience is the moment you choose to surrender to God. From that point, all of heaven, all that will ever be required to live a life of Christ is in you, now.

Do not stop there! There is *so much more* to a life in Christ Jesus that will take you further through life, successfully as you grow. Growth is the sign of change. You will change, as you grow in Christ. If nothing is changing in you, **examine yourself.**

Invite the searchlight of the Holy Spirit to shed light on the hidden things that keep you snared. It is one step toward freedom from the past: one step toward your new life.

Show sincerity, by continuing in your pursuit to fulfill God's plan for you, and the Lord will bless you. I pray heart boldness and faith-filled courage to stand against the wiles and strategies of the wicked one; to resist the sin that so easily ensnares you.

Be active in the Gifts of the Holy Spirit, as outlined in His Word (First Corinthians 12). Learn to do your own digging into the Word of God, and He will truly show you things to come.

We are assured great demonstrations of God's word and Power if we only believe. To believe Him, you must first know Him. Become personally acquainted with the Lord. Holiness, holy living, holy expressions of love, faith and hope are part of our lives, to be experienced in growing depths and dimensions, as we seek and inquire the Lord out of pure love and necessity. We are, I believe, among the last of all generations that will live to see the return of the Lord.

It has fallen to us, the responsibility to teach what we know to be true. To withhold information that could set another person free from pain, bondage, and defeat, is cruel and unusual; even sinful. Many of us as leaders of churches have the vital lifesaving, life changing,

life altering information of Spiritual Warfare, and we are doing nothing with it. Like the man who hid his talent; will the Lord return to find you have done nothing with the gift?

If you think avoiding the subject of spiritual warfare will lessen adversity and lighten spiritual battles, you are in deception. All you have managed to accomplish is a lack of resistance to the devil, a lack of submission to God, and an accumulation of demons that will not flee. **Get delivered!**

Rise up! Take your position and stand and see the delivering power of His hand move in your life, in your family and *in your church,* in Jesus' Name.

Spiritual Warfare:

*It's about the **fight;** it's about the **freedom,***
*and it's about the **fire** of God,*
in the life of <u>every child of God.</u>

If you are not fighting, you are not free. If you are
not free, you are not on fire for God! Fight for
someone; Free someone! Fire them up for God!

Continue to make progress, and to grow in the gifts and callings of God.

Get busy about your Father's business,
in setting captives free and
WATCH GOD MOVE!

SECTION THREE

The Fire: Holiness

I used to think, as a young believer, that holiness meant **boring**, and was reserved for **old people.** I was **so** wrong! Discovering the untapped treasure of holiness, opened wide the doors of opportunity to see demonstrations of God's presence, *like never.*

Evil is exposed by holiness.

Holiness is the one characteristic of God, where the miracles happen. Demons yield to the Holiness of God, and some have been cast out screaming simply by the subtle movement of God's fiery holiness. It is a characteristic that God's people are invited to strive to achieve, instructed to put on, live by and abide in. It is achievable. It is attainable.

It is a weapon of war, for me.

The holiness of God is the fire of His Spirit. It burns the chaff, and the waste places; exposes, sifts, and analyzes the thoughts and intentions of hearts; God's holiness.

It is *pure.* It is *love.* It is *God.*

No evil can stand in the presence of a Holy God. When that same Holy God lives in you, expresses Himself through you, touches and reaches lost and suffering, dying humanity through you, you *can rest assured* great power will be released through you *as well*, power from heaven.

Revelation comes through holiness. From time spent building on your relationship with God, you find important information being revealed to you, that brings direction, strength, confirmation, hope and healing to God's people.

Reach for holy living, *in the Lord.*

Be in His presence, *deliberately.*

It is the *key* to deliverance.

9

THE SPIRIT OF FAITH
VS
THE SPIRIT OF FEAR

God's word is clear about faith and fear. It is the absolute strength of our being, for a Christian who taps into the power of faith and the *gift of faith*, spoken of in the Scriptures. Faith is the absence of fear, considering the Presence of God, for me. When I put my mind and heart on the Lord, fear is gone. Only faith remains.

These two, faith and fear, are absolute opposites, completely antagonistic of the other, and true enemies of one and another. To *be afraid* is a natural response and nothing to be afraid of *to remain fearful* is **not a natural response** for someone who believes in God, *but it does happen.* We must deal with the source of our fears, and the issue of our faith. Our goal as a Christian is to grow in our faith, and it happens in stages; baby steps, at first.

With faith its **first, baby steps**, *then baby runs! Your walk with God throughout your life in Christ, grows strong!* Challenges in life, are opportunities to grow in faith, and to draw close to God. Faith increases, while fear fades away.

Faith strengthens, while fear weakens.

For months now, probably close to a year I began to dig deep into studying the spiritual root cause of sickness and disease. During that journey, I grew particularly interested in the brain and more particularly the **hypothalamic gland.** It is the gland, near the pituitary gland which *controls, facilitates, and issues orders to the rest of the body, which in turn reacts either to fear, or to faith.*

This gland <u>responds</u> to *thoughts.* Depending on your thoughts, whether of stress, fear, anxiety, etc., secretions of hormones are released that immediately connect to your Central Nervous System. Those secretions *result* in a flight or fight response, that races through our Central Nervous System, and our body is on alert.

Another thing I found interesting is how this gland is the Direct Affecter to our male or female organs, and all other vital organs in the body.

... in other words, the signals from our Central Nervous System race to these primary organs immediately and the stress builds up in them. Our organs were not intended or designed to be in constant stress, on constant alert, or in constant rigidity from tensions building up from the thoughts that fill our mind. God's word says, **"Great Peace** *have they, whose mind stays on Thee" (Isaiah 26:3).* The devil does not want you to have the Great Peace God's word promises, so the battle to keep our attention on the pain that surrounds us, or our loved ones intensifies. Fixation on the things that are outside of our control is a very strong weapon the enemy of your soul uses, often. The soul is the mind, will and

emotions. The eyes are the windows to the soul. Your soul will reflect, your life will reflect those very things that consume our thought life. What are your eyes on? What is your mind filled with? That is what your life will reflect.

If your eyes are not on the Lord, you are going to struggle much more than you should have to.
*It is the **Spirit of our Mind** that must have <u>continual renewing</u> from the <u>constant bombarding</u> of life situations, alone. Add to that inner turmoil, inner conflict that we as people go through, in trying to find our place in this world.*

Without God in your life, you are LOST!

Fear fights to keep a hold on you. It is a very strong spirit, with a very loud voice; but not **too much for God.** Fear can web its way through to every fiber of your being, therefore binding, and weakening you, an opportunity for sickness. Our bodies react to fear, to the threat of attack; to the stress and tensions that come from continual fearfulness. **Faith in God**, and in His ability to come through for you, to bring you and those you love all the way through troubling situations **and out,** is where the power of _**faith**_ can be found.

The battle for control of your thoughts, is between you and the devil. The good news is, you have given control over to the Lord and that is who the devil must deal with, when your mind is fixed on Him. Pull your thoughts over to God when the heat of the battle rises. When you are in the fiery *heat* of bombardments that fill your mind with fear, anger, or confusion. Pull your mind over to the Lord and His ability to rescue and redeem the situation, in a way that leads to peace. It is the place of battle, and it is the place of victory, for the child of God: **the mind.**

If you want to see victory, if you want to experience breakthrough, *take hold of your mind,* and *submit it to God.* That filthy thing needs washing, needs renewing, and needs to be cleansed in the Blood of Jesus. Renew your mind with the washing of the Word of God, and faith will COME ALIVE!

Do not be like most *Christians* who talk about their faith but have nothing to show for it, nor any power of God being demonstrated through their lives. People like that fade out. Ministries like that die away. Preachers like that retire for lack of *fire, in their faith.*

Be like the few who do not have to talk about the faith they have in God, you can see it by how they live, trusting the Lord for each day, and each day's provision. Those who appear to be poor, by the worlds' measure, are so rich in their faith in God!

People who do not back away at impossible situations but address those impossibilities by the God Who RULES over every impossibility, activating their faith in Him and in His Word, *are those we should learn from.*

Walk a life of faith, and the Lord will show Himself mighty on your behalf. He will go before you and open wide the way of escape; the way to blessings money cannot buy.

When

faith ~vs~ fear,

faith rules!

10

PUT ON THE
FULL ARMOR OF GOD

I *love* the covering of the Lord. I have a fresh and new, very recent appreciation for it, and desire to learn more about the covering God makes readily available to us, and the urgent, very important reason found in the Scriptures concerning it.

God's word on the Armor of God:

Ephesians 6:13-17

"Therefore, put on the full armor of God, so that when the day of evil comes, you may be able to stand your ground, and after you have done everything, to stand. Stand firm then, with the belt of truth buckled around your waist, with the breastplate of righteousness in place, and with your feet fitted with the readiness that comes from the gospel of peace. In addition to all this, take up the shield of faith, with which you can extinguish all the flaming arrows of the evil one. Take the helmet of salvation and the sword of the Spirit, which is the Word of God."

In this Chapter, I want to highlight and emphasize the various parts of the Armor of God and hope to expand your scope of awareness and information, on this very important subject.

I also want to bring to light, a piece of the armor,

never mentioned in modern teachings or sermons. It is a piece of armor that must come to the forefront in the life of a child of God especially those engaged in spiritual warring.

There is another piece of armor worn by mounted warriors who were about to engage in battle, as history teaches. No warrior was found without this battle piece. The armor piece known as a lance is, for some reason, skipped over in the listing of articles that make up the armor of God, in the Bible. But this piece has a very significant role.

The Lance...

A lance is a pole weapon or spear designed to be used by a mounted warrior, according to Wikipedia. It is used to pierce and cut through.

Recently, in the middle of a Prophetic Conference here in Texas the Word of the Lord came to a woman, which spoke of a *lance.*

The Lord was showing us how this woman had been praying for so long, concerning the men in her family whom she loved dearly. She had been praying in every way she knew how to pray, and for so long but it had been as if she had never been able to **make contact.**

The Lord went on to show how her loved ones were as if, on one end of a great, divided valley. I heard the word "chasm" and "gulf". And that she was on the other side sending prayers, with such *force of thrust and accuracy,* by and through her

Intercession. The Lord went on to show us all, that **the force of thrust and accuracy <u>in sending</u>** the Word of God in prayer, was like the lance in the hands of a FULLY armored, fully EQUIPPED man or woman of God. The Lord reminded us, through this Word, that the lance was part of our armor when **we send the Word of God** *in the power of the Holy Spirit, through continual prayers of intercession.* The force and accuracy of the **sent Word of God,** over our loved ones will make contact where we cannot and will *pierce the enemy who rides the back of our loved ones.*

This is only a part, a very important part of how God provides covering for us through the equipping of **force and power** behind our prayers. The force and power of heaven!

The armor of God is the covering of our mind, heart, walk and life *before God and man,* and the active authority to demonstrate God's power on the earth, as a result. The armor of God *is Jesus!*

1. **Belt of Truth:** The first element of the armor is Truth, which contradicts Satan's lies. Knowing the Truth of Who God is and who we are in Christ, is first and foremost in importance, when engaging in spiritual warfare. Truth sets us apart. Truth is deliverance. You shall know the Truth, and the Truth will make you free. Jesus Christ is Truth.

2. **Breastplate of Righteousness:** Shielding our vital organs from deadly blows, a warrior could not enter the battle without his breastplate. This piece of armor for a Christian, **is not**

works of righteousness or good deeds. It is the righteousness of Christ, imputed by God and received by faith, **guarding our hearts** against the Accuser. Being right with God and knowing it in your heart, protects your life from evil being able to succeed against you.

3. **Shoes of Peace:** Get your steps and direct your aim for spiritual conflict, *in readiness.* Ability to overcome obstacles along the path, intended to delay the advancement of God's will, comes from a surefooted child of God. Traps and snares are avoided by the *surefooted* child of God who is *ready, willing, and able to advance* God's Kingdom, in setting people free with the Gospel of Peace. The steps of the righteous are ordered of the Lord, and the victory in Christ is ours to be realized! A man or woman of God who has the Peace of God in their walk is a fierce weapon in the hands of the Lord.

4. **Shield of Faith:** Nullifies all forms of doubt about God, His Word or Faithfulness. This article of protection keeps us from trusting, depending, or relying on ourselves or in others. Words and doubtful situations aimed to deter you from God's narrow path, **ricochet off** the Shield of Faith.

5. **Helmet of Salvation:** Preserving our thought life and keeping the seat of our mind in God. Capable of discerning and distinguishing between truth and deception. This armor keeps your mind fixed on Christ. This piece of armor provides protection, by the knowledge of God.

Knowing who you are in Christ, is protection from defeat.

6. **Sword of the Spirit:** The only offensive weapon of the whole armor: *the holiness and power of the Word of God.* It is the weapon used by Jesus when Satan *tempted Him* in the desert wilderness. Do not even imagine having this article of God's armor with little or no personal study of God's word. Fresh Word is a Sharp Sword!

7. **Pray in the Spirit:** With the mind of Christ and His heart and priorities. This is by and through the baptism of the Holy Spirit, the infilling of God's presence in your life. To put on the armor of God, is to **put on Christ;** Before the Scriptures reveal anything about any of the armor, God's word says to put it on because the day of evil is coming...

*"Therefore, **put on the full armor of God, so that when the day of evil comes, you may be able to stand your ground**... verse 13.*

Your relationship with God, *with Jesus Christ* is the **most important part of your armor,** *your covering.* **Days of evil are here** and more are to come. Will you be able to stand your ground, in the Lord, on that evil day? Put on Jesus, and do not take Him off!

11

THE POWER OF THE BLOOD OF JESUS CHRIST

When reduced to one drop of blood, that *one drop of blood* is ALL IT TAKES to cancel the works, assignments, and efforts of the devil himself, **if that blood is the Blood of our Lord and Savior, Jesus Christ.**

Without repeating very important information that is already available regarding the power of the Blood of Christ, I want to instead impart some information on this subject, from another perspective: **from the perspective of firsthand experience, *by testimony.***

We overcome by the Blood of the Lamb and by the word of our testimony. Rev. 12:11

Soon after giving our lives over to the Lordship of Jesus Christ, it was as if we were immediately thrust into a world consisting of great spiritual matters, and the subject of great spiritual wars. Wars that, if not won in the realm or dimension of the spirit by effective prayer and intercession, result in great, adverse physical situations.

Situations we find our children in, *may have been deterred* and even thwarted by the effective prayers of the righteous man or woman of God...

according to the Word of God.

Situations concerning our marriage and relationships have become chaotic, *because of a failure in enduring* the long-suffering travail, required by effective prayer and intercession.

I do not believe in praying outside the boundaries of the Blood of Jesus Christ. Even speaking strategically, outside of the boundaries of His Powerful Blood, I have come to avoid.

My conversations with God, I now cover in the Blood of Jesus, when I pray. Some say it sounds extreme... I say, *"IT WORKS!"*

It has been *by and through* the power of the Blood of Jesus that every single weapon, assignment, and effort of evil made against me has been brought to nothing. They have all been cancelled, never to rise again a second time... (Nahum 1:9).

Death sentences cancelled by the Blood of Jesus.

Divorce cancelled by the Blood of Jesus.

Depression cancelled by the Blood of Jesus.

His Blood rescues from the valley of the shadow of death, rescues from the snare of the fowler and the noisome pestilence... protects from the threat of attack.

No disorder, no sin, no aggravation, or divisiveness can continue its hold when the Blood of Jesus covers you!

Demons FLEE at the mention of the Blood of Jesus Christ.

I have had witches walk right into my church and stand right next to me, and literally squirm, itch, scratch and FLEE as fast as they could, when I WHISPERED the power of the Blood of Jesus... *at the mere whisper!*

We have had practicing witches pour ceremonial powders and headless birds on our church porch to stop the move of God on our lives... those two people are dead today. The exact spells they were casting on us, came upon their own heads (Psalm 109:17).

I know of a witch, *a family witch* who cursed a daughter in law with throat cancer. This daughter-in-law was a Christian! God healed and protected the daughter-in-law, and suddenly the witch herself was stricken with throat cancer in less than a year! The daughter in law, *WHO KNEW* what this woman had done, led the witch mother-in-law to the Lord, on her deathbed hours before she died. That witch was my husband's grandmother.

The Bible says, *those that love cursing, it will come upon their own heads* (Psalm 109:17).

That is the power of the Blood of Jesus.

My husband and I have walked into the ICU Unit with a person given less than 3 weeks to live from lung cancer. This woman and her husband were not saved. As I was speaking to them about the miracle working power of God, faith and the subject of healing, a nurse with a red dot on her forehead walked in and overheard my clergy/patient conversation, and with a sudden outburst said, "ha! *God* doesn't do miracles; you all are always talking *miracles, miracles, miracles...*", when something rose up in me and I turned to her and said, "the power of the Blood of Jesus is against you devil" and the nurse ran out!

The patient was in her own room in three days and released to go home by the third week! After the nurse ran out, we ministered salvation and they requested another nurse. When you need a miracle, do not surround yourself with a bunch of godless, criticizing doubters, who do not know the Miracle Worker. This woman was healed!

That is the power of the Blood of Jesus!

Years ago, in the mid ninety's we were pastoring in our first location and experiencing many supernatural experiences in our services. A prophetic word came forth at the end of a regular Sunday morning service, where people received physically, during the time of greatest anointing.

The prophetic word was in how the people, who had just witnessed some great things, were about to witness faith and to witness more of God's miracle working power. Within half an hour or so, church was dismissed and the people began to exit the church. With just a few people left in the sanctuary, whom my husband and I were ministering to privately and personally, we suddenly heard horrible screams coming from outside the front exit areas of the church.

Immediately, people began to run into the church screaming, as my husband and I, and those with us in the room began to run toward the screams. Making our way out of the building and racing through parked cars, (our church was a storefront), we ran toward a parked van that was in the middle of the street.

Everyone was running away from the van and the street, and to the church sidewalk; my husband and I, with our head usher at the time behind us, ran toward the front of the van, a Dodge Ram Van, to see the mangled body of a child, twisted and with her eyes wide open, faced down on the hot summer, street.

Her face was toward us, her wide eyes in a blank stare of shock. Running toward her body I saw the tire tracks from the ¾ ton van, up the back of her torn shirt running to the base of her head. Her leg was bent at the knee and twisted all the way in the opposite direction, as if snapped. Her hair nearly covered her entire face. I fell to my knees, and gently slid my hands under her face to get it off the hot street. *And I spoke to the Lord.*

Our head usher took his coat to cover her little body. There was no sign of life. She was not breathing. She made no sound. There was no movement. Time stood still.

And I spoke to the Lord.

My husband went to the parents. People were screaming everywhere; wails reached the heavens as the horror of the moment seized the minds and hearts of people who came to see what was happening.

And I spoke to the Lord.

All I could say was not even a prayer as some would define a prayer. I said, as I slid my hands between her face and the hot street, took her face into my hands and whispered into her ear, *"Lord the Blood of Jesus covers her, in the Name of Jesus. This baby has been singing to You all day. She has been coloring pages for You and in Your Name all morning. The Blood of Jesus covers her..."*

I could hear the devastation coming from the crowd. I could hear the prayers of some and could feel a sense of shielding or covering over the area where she lay, and **still could hear *no ambulance*** *from the Fire Station that was only two blocks away.*

I reminded the Lord of what I had seen her doing in class that morning, her singing, her dancing, her joy!

Suddenly and without warning she lifted her head and forced out a whimpering cry for her daddy, AS HER LEG SNAPPED BACK INTO PLACE.

The people screamed as I helped her lay back down, when the sound of Life Flight came through in the far distance, and the sound of an ambulance drew near. We managed to get the daddy to collect himself enough to draw near to his baby and help calm her to stay still.

Paramedics arriving, I moved out of the way, and making my way toward my husband who stood near the van, I saw where her hair was *caught* around the headlight. As it happened, she had stepped out, into the path of the oncoming vehicle, while holding her mama's hand. She darted out in front of it, just enough for it to clip her and drag her several yards, catching hold of her shirt or something; the van dragged her, and had to go in reverse to get it off her.

But because of the Blood of Jesus! She was released from the hospital that same night with only a bruised lung and other minor injuries!

That is the power of the Blood of Jesus*!*

When my eldest daughter's obstetrician told her, something was wrong with her unborn baby; when the Cat Scan, *(which I still have),* showed only a ¾ formation of the brain, and other test results *(which I still have),* showed traces of Trisomy 18*... and she was advised to abort, we called upon the Power of the Blood of Jesus.

That was over 20 years ago and my granddaughter is healthy, receiving her diploma early! Today, she is the mother of my first *great* grandchild! Just imagine the opposite being true, had we not leaned on the Lord and fully trusted Him.

She herself now overcomes downfalls, temptations, shortcomings, and issues in life by the same power of God that brought her through the first time, while she was still in the womb of her mother!

One month of solid spiritual warfare produced a CLEAR and NORMAL CATSCAN! Calling upon the faithfulness of God, calling on God's mercy to come through for my unsaved daughter and unborn grandchild! And God came through for her, faithful to the Blood of Christ!

That is the power of the Blood of Jesus*!*

Protection. Salvation. Deliverance. Freedom. More than anything you could ever imagine, hope for or dream of; the strength and All-Powerful Blood that Christ shed on the cross is alive and available to us all, today.

There is a freedom that comes from knowing your life is covered, immersed, soaked, and saturated by the Blood of the Lord Jesus Christ.

The spirit of death itself cannot prevail against you and must *Passover* you, due to the Blood of Jesus Christ. The power of the Blood of Jesus, no devil can withstand. By His Blood, *death and death sentences* are cancelled, and brought to nothing. Curses are broken and destroyed and affliction is done away with.

Nahum 1:9, "I will make a full end; affliction will not rise up again, a second time".

It is what preserves our loved ones, protecting and bringing them through until they decide for Christ. It is His Undeserved Mercy because He is not willing that any would perish.

Yes, the power of the Blood of Jesus will preserve your loved ones, as the Lord is not wanting of them to die in their sin; His blood keeps them.

Only the Blood of Jesus is powerful enough to wash away the sin and its *stainful* residue. The effects of sin and sinfulness are destroyed by the Blood of the Lamb.

*Trisomy 18 is a genetic disorder that includes a combination of birth defects. This includes severe intellectual disability, as well as health problems involving nearly every organ system in the body. Most babies born with trisomy 18 die by age 1.

12

THE POWER OF HIS NAME

More and more, with every passing day and every passing challenge there is demonstration of one thing for the child of God: *the absolute defeat of the workings of evil assignments, when we hold to, and exercise the Power of the Name of Jesus Christ.*

The very first time I experienced this Truth for myself, was just after turning my life over to the Lord.

I was fresh *out of* witchcraft, **but not out of sin.** The devil was **not about** to let me go *without a fight*, but this time when the attack came *something was different.*

I had been baptized in the Holy Ghost. The difference now, was I belonged to Jesus and was **Blood bought**, Holy Ghost filled and speaking in tongues.

It was exactly three weeks after receiving Christ and renouncing witchcraft, sin, and everything about it. I had gotten rid of everything about sin and everything that went with it... **except my live-in boyfriend,** *(now husband).*

Anyone who has encountered a **physical,** *spiritual attack* will know that what I am describing is demonic, *and very real.* If all your doors are shut *but one*, trust that the enemy who comes to steal, kill, and destroy will come right-in, through that very door every time. Late one night for me, was that time.

Laying on my bed, facing my bedroom door with only a hint of closet light on, I saw a black form enter my room, *and come straight for me.* I had been a practicing witch for some time before this and was aware of what this was.

I was saved now, though. I was a Christian. I was baptized in the Holy Spirit and had renounced my involvement in the occult just three weeks prior. My salvation experience was fresh and new; **but I had NOT** *let go of the way* **the devil kept** *coming back* **into my life...** *my compromise.*

I was living with a man I was not married to. Common Law is not common with God. The Lord does not wink at this sin which opens the door to Ungodly Soul Ties, highlighted earlier.

So, I lay wake up in bed, not sure why, but facing my bedroom door, when I saw the *form* enter.

It looked like a large, wide cloud of dark muffler smoke, only it moved and had form to it; *it was the size of a full-grown man and it was moving toward me.*

As I turned abruptly to my left, to wake up my *sleeping, live-in boyfriend and man I was not married to in God's eyes, but would not leave because he loved me,* I was literally and forcefully yanked back, **flat.** Immediately I **physically felt** and *audibly heard,* a *"coiling hiss"* wrap speedily and forcefully from my head to my toes. My arms were motionless beside me and I could not speak. I could not move my tongue. I could not swallow. I could not whisper my boyfriend's name, who was right next to me...

I was completely paralyzed, except for my thoughts, and all I could "hear" was the word "rape, rape, rape, rape" racing through my mind.

The weapon was being formed against me.

I was a Christian. I was a Christian with an open door, and a rolled out welcome mat called **compromise** which is the same as giving the devil **permission to attack!**

Common Law *is not* common with God.

I clearly remember the weight of this devil, *as if that of a person,* begin to weigh me down...

But I had the Holy Ghost!

This time I had an *infilling* of God's **unmistakable power** rising in me.

Physically, the sensation was like the bubbling of seltzer water, *but it was rising <u>in me</u> and I was fully aware of it.* The moment the *"bubbling"* reached my vocal cords I experienced a BURST of power rush with force out of my mouth, and I *yelled* the Name, ***Jesus!***

As fast as that devil came in, it fled at the Name of my Jesus.

My life would never be the same. I had been baptized in the ***knowledge*** <u>*of the power*</u> of His

Name. It was as if I was <u>now equipped</u> with a weapon called **the knowledge of the power** of the Name of Jesus, through this experience. I shared the experience fully in my book, [1]INCEST: The Curse of Destruction...Reversed.

There would be many more experiences like that one, but this ONE changed my prayer life!

I raise the covering banner of the Name of the Lord, over my family and loved ones, daily in intercessory prayer. I have come to learn that His Name is a shielding force from evil that waits to seize our families; that fights ruthlessly to keep them from turning to the Lord.

Often, it is as if the more I pray, the worse it gets; and the devil would love for me to stop praying, as if that would make him stop attacking the ones I love so dearly. The devil is a liar and the father of all lies, and in him there is no truth.

"He was a murderer from the beginning, not holding to the truth, for there is no truth in him. When he lies, he speaks his native language, for he is a liar and the father of lies," (John 8:44)

When I *do not* know what to do; when I *do not* know how to pray, I whisper the Name that is above ALL Names, Jesus! and His presence comes on the scene. God's presence *fills me* with faith, hope and evidence of God's love for m e and those I pray for.

When the enemy turns up the heat of adversity

---

[1] www.amazon.com/INCEST-Destruction-REVERSED-Overcomers-Testimony/dp/0964364905/ref=tmm_pap_swatch_0?_encoding=UTF8&qid=&sr=

against you and those you love, YOU TURN UP THE HEAT by persevering in the Name of Jesus.

Endure in your stand against the adversary, by the power of the Name of Jesus. His Name is strength for the battle. His Name brings you through your valleys of decision and troubling. His Name is health and healing for your life! Wrap yourself up in the beauty and healing of His Name! Ask Him to infuse you with revelation of the fullness of that power. His Name is ALL-POWERFUL and we need to access the benefit of that Name.

I have been standing in the gap, through prayers and intercession for over 30 years in some cases, for a loved one who is lost and undone without God. Enduring strength comes from His Name! Protection and Preservation come from the covering of His Name. I believe it is solely due to the Name of Jesus, that my loved ones have been preserved from more horrible outcomes, and even death!

Our son survived a four-time roll over vehicle accident that slammed into a tree over eight feet in the air, with no oxygen for nearly thirty minutes while the Jaws of Life extracted him, *died* during Life Flight, *on* the operating table, *and two months later* in a bloody attack made against his life!

While his left arm was DEAD from the accident, and PARTIAL SKULL removed from brain surgery, *he was sliced open with a razor blade* to the bone of his right arm, just below the elbow! The surgeon called it *"filet"* to the bone; all tendons, ligaments, everything.

My son not only survived by the power of God, but fully recovered all use of his arms and graduated with a degree in carpentry!

That is the power of the Name of Jesus!

I make it my goal to pause before the Lord and remind myself of my need of His inclusion when facing *battles, storms, challenges, and decisions, when peace is far from me.*

When the phone call came in that told me my youngest son was facing nearly forty years for a non-violent crime. He was 25 years old.

My son is home now, because of the power of the Name of Jesus, *after two years!*

Yes, our loved ones do things that open the door to the devil of disaster, but YOUR PRAYERS OF INTERCESSION in the *NAME OF JESUS*, will protect them from dying in their sin, until they make it right with God! When others criticize, YOU PRAY! God will respond to *your prayers!*

I make it my goal to *lean into* the Name of the Lord, for wisdom and to guide and protect me... to keep me in all my ways; **some say** *I lean too much* on Him, but I do not care about *"some say-ers"*, I only care that **He responds!**

God will always respond to the Name of Jesus. The angels of God respond to the Name of Jesus. Demons bow their knee to the Name of Jesus.

There will come a day, I believe we will see during our lifetime, and in the span of the lifetime of our grandchildren where we will witness DROVES of people surrendering their lives over to the Lordship of Jesus Christ and will choose to live according to His power and authority. I believe it will be due to the evil that is about to be unleashed on the earth.

Great evil is already seeping through over our world, over our land... not far from our neighborhoods and schools. We have seen an accelerated evil literally loosed, and unshackled, with human sacrifices being televised all over the world, as the time of Satan draws near. There is more to come.

Do not wait for more to come. Today is the day given to us, to choose to live for God.

A Great Day of Choosing is not too far away.

We will be in this warfare until the Lord returns for us, *for His church.* I pray you make it your aim, to live for God; to strive for *the full equipping* that it will take to overcome this present evil.

Our children and theirs will only know what scriptural truths we teach them. The world is full of watered-down doctrine, powerless churches, and defeated Christians. Pulpits are manned by sinister ministers; carnal, self-serving messengers who fail to teach God's people where to find biblical truths in the word of God, to defeat the work of evil. They do not want people offended right out the door, along with their wallets.

Where will our loved ones go?

Many will not hear us, until it is too late. Will you leave them the keys, that will unlock the doors of great spiritual victory; to witness great demonstrations of the faithfulness of God to deliver from evil? Will you leave them the keys to the only freedom God has assured us of?

When you are gone to be with the Lord, *how* will they ever know the miracle working power of God that you know to be true?

We hold the keys.

9 Keys to Effective Spiritual Warfare

Thirty years have passed, and a whole lot of accumulated "hit-and-miss" prayers have been sent through the heavenlies, only to continue their flight through endless horizons of deep space. Carnal prayers of panic, desperation, doubt, and well-wishing never really find their way to the throne room of God, I am afraid.

Finally, though, I have settled in my mind and heart, that those who have gone before me, <u>pioneering paths of prayers to God and achieving great results</u>, must have a special connection to Him! They must KNOW something or HAVE something that I do not. *Keys, perhaps?* And they know how to use them!

Here is a short list, I have comprised in hope of helping those who find themselves praying, and achieving little or nothing, as a result. Outside of "writing on the Lord's 'perfect timing', there is little else one can do. Use this short list to help evaluate whether you are in the 'waiting on God' season, or just stuck!

1. **Know the Power of your God, and Father** and His willingness to come through for you, and those you pray for. Peace to endure the battle, and ward off battle fatigue will follow.

2. **Know the Season** in which you are standing, currently. Strategy will come. Strategic insight will come that can be included in your prayer. Confidence creates *a heart of gratitude,* a *shift* in the force of your prayer to God, unleashing the power of a merciful Father.

3. **Look for the timing of God,** as you pray. He often *quickens* you to know *'duration'.* You will need patience, endurance, strength, and the knowledge of long suffering, *in your stand.* Experience provides that. Pull from the resource of your experience with the God and Father of perfect timing. The on-time God! You will need to know times and seasons, and how the Lord takes people through them, often with only your Intercessory Prayers preserving and sustaining them.

4. **Recognize the enemy of *"Routine"*, and *"Limitation"*,** and distance yourself from it. Nothing will douse out the fire of God faster than routine, or doubt. Doubt puts limits on God and is a step away from fear. Faith filled prayers, are not prayers that conform or settle for the easy way out. Faith filled prayers are out of the ordinary and will stretch you beyond the limits you have become comfortably familiar with.

5. **Identify Distractors:** Increase deliberate self-discipline, in maintaining momentum, consistency, and achieving prayerful outcomes that usher in healing, comfort, liberty, and life

transforming salvation. Distractions are an enemy in spiritual warfare. Eliminating them causes the effectiveness needed in spiritual warfare. It offers the spiritual fine-tuning needed to hear and align yourself in prayer with the Lord and His will, concerning the issues we face in prayer.

6. **Identify Points of Entry:** Close, Remove and Eliminate means of access to the enemy, by both word *(prayer),* and deed *(action)*. We do our part, as the Lord leads and He will do His part (what we cannot do), all the while maintaining prayer. How is the devil getting through to your loved one? Through anger, sickness, recklessness? A deaf and dumb spirit? In prayer, shut those doors. In prayer, shield and protect your loved ones with a thick hedge of God's word. In action, let those loved ones know you are praying and not going to stop. Nothing will go right for anyone not aligned with the will of God for their lives when Effective Spiritual Warfare is at work. People are out of timing, out of step, out of alignment with the Lord and have STOPPED living for Him, ***key point of entry.***

7. **Fully Utilize the Word of God**, in your prayer and petition. Skim off verbiage, and unnecessary wordage in prayer. Fine Tune your prayer by adopting the use of *praying the Word of God. Choosing to pray the Word of God stored up in your spirit man,* over the use of words that fill your mind and have been memorized, is *all powerful.*

8. **Eliminate Vain Repetition.** Pray the "sticking points", and make clear your definite, specific request, *your need.* Praying the specific Scriptures that pertain directly to your situation of need, will eliminate vain repetition in prayer. Vain Repetition is a *form of godliness*, producing no power.

9. **Know the Will of God** for the situation. This comes from spending time: quality, undiluted, uninterrupted, precious time in an atmosphere that promotes stillness before the Lord, confidence, and fervency.

10. **Did I say nine? Walk in the Spirit,** and you will not give flesh, or carnality, a place in your prayers. Promptings from God are not the same as impulses from the flesh/emotion of man. There is a very distinct difference that can only be detected in the spirit, by your relationship with the Lord.

Of course, this is only a short list of keys' that will help keep you on the victorious side of Effective Spiritual Warfare. *Reminding ourselves* that others, as well as our own specific needs are <u>worth fighting for in vigorous, fervent even violent prayer before the Lord</u>, *helps promote motivation.*

Motivation strengthens us three-fold: *Spirit, Soul and Body.* By this we go from the simplicity and more *laxed* position of a prayer partner, into the rewarding prayer-filled life of an Intercessor, skillful in Effective Spiritual Warfare. Intercessors pray you all the way through to victory no matter how long it takes.

"He who has believed and has been baptized shall be saved; but he who has not believed shall be condemned (to hell). Mark 16:16

These signs will accompany
<u>*those who have believed:*</u>

<u>*In my Name,*</u> **they will** *cast out devils,*
they will *speak with new tongues;* **they will**
pick up serpents and if they drink anything
deadly, it will not hurt them; **they will** *lay*
hands on the sick, and the sick shall recover."
Mark 16: 17-18

THE WORDS OF JESUS

ABOUT THE AUTHOR

Sandra was ordained through the laying on of hands, by the ministry of the late John Osteen of Lakewood Church, Houston, TX., in the early '90's. She has appeared on the 700 Club and HEART TO HEART with contemporary Christian Music Artist and Author, Sheila Walsh, Daystar's Taking a Break with Joni Lamb and more. **Her ministry** of *"healing through forgiveness"* exposes the snare of bitterness brought forth through sexual assault as a child, sexual assault as a teen, domestic violence, drug and alcohol addiction, suicide as well as the occult... all of which the power of God has freed her from. **Her story** of God's *healing and delivering power* has continued to inspire people around the world. She is a public speaker, and ministers in the five-fold ministry anointing with strengths in prophetic spiritual warfare and evangelism.

She is an author and publisher, creative visionary & executive producer for The Mary Magdalene Project: A book/film project on the life of Mary Magdalene. Sandra is the Founding Pastor of New Life Ministries, serving as Pastor and Director of Ministries. She is the pioneer for the *Gathering of Warriors Crusades,* in Texas, and **Emerge**, *a ministry to the broken in development for streamlined viewing.*

She and her family live near Houston, Texas, pastoring with her warrior husband of 30+ years.

ABOUT THE MINISTRY

NEW LIFE MINISTRIES reaches out to hurting people trapped by the shadows of their past and is a ministry to the backslider. As pastors their work has included successful at-risk youth programs and Texas crusades, such as the **Gathering of Warriors,** where a powerful demonstration of the Holy Spirit fills the atmosphere and whereby lives are dramatically changed.

Through the prophetic spiritual warfare mantle on this ministry, people are set free to the glory of God. They continue in home-church, publishing, media and filmmaking.

In development are Mary Magdalene, the film and Emerge, a ministry to the broken. Emerge is accepting testimonials for inclusion to their streaming YouTube program, in Development.

New Life Publishing and New Life Media are extensions of New Life Ministries.

For more, see:

www.NewLifeMinistryMedia.com

On YouTube at youtube.com/alandsandracerda

CONTACT & RESOURCES

Available for Public Speaking & Ministry.

Email:
TheMaryMagdaleneProject@gmail.com

For more on Sandra Cerda, visit the website at
www.SandraCerda.com

More Titles at Amazon/Books/SandraCerda

Mary Magdalene: *A Historic Novel*
Mary Magdalene *Study-Guide*
Mary Magdalene: *The Play*
and more in the Mary Magdalene Series

See **www.MaryMagdalene.Film** for
More on The Mary Magdalene Project
On Face Book @*MaryMagdaleneFilm*

Water Me, *Lord! (Devotional Journal)*

INCEST: The Curse of Destruction...*Reversed!*
(Autobiography)

The Fortified Marriage Series:
Love Me Knots: *Binding Wisdom For A Strong Marriage*
Love Me Knots: *When The Tempter Comes*
Love Me Knots: *Intimate Issues*

Spiritual Warfare: *The Fight, The Freedom, The Fire*

Dream Peace: *When God Speaks*
(Bible-Based Dream Interpretation)

New Life Publishing

Bringing 1st Time Authors to Print!

On Facebook @1st Time Authors

www.ingramcontent.com/pod-product-compliance
Lightning Source LLC
LaVergne TN
LVHW041223080426
835508LV00011B/1053